MARCUS C THOMAS

Witch of the Mountain

The Real Story of Granny Dollar

First published by Marcus C. Thomas 2021

Copyright © 2021 by Marcus C Thomas

All rights reserved. No part of this publication may be reproduced, stored or transmitted in any form or by any means, electronic, mechanical, photocopying, recording, scanning, or otherwise without written permission from the publisher. It is illegal to copy this book, post it to a website, or distribute it by any other means without permission.

Marcus C Thomas asserts the moral right to be identified as the author of this work.

Marcus C Thomas has no responsibility for the persistence or accuracy of URLs for external or third-party Internet Websites referred to in this publication and does not guarantee that any content on such Websites is, or will remain, accurate or appropriate.

Designations used by companies to distinguish their products are often claimed as trademarks. All brand names and product names used in this book and on its cover are trade names, service marks, trademarks and registered trademarks of their respective owners. The publishers and the book are not associated with any product or vendor mentioned in this book. None of the companies referenced within the book have endorsed the book.

First edition

ISBN: 978-0-578-84610-1

Editing by Stacci P. Thomas
Editing by Shannon Dell
Advisor: Lisa Thomas

This book was professionally typeset on Reedsy.
Find out more at reedsy.com

To Lisa, my life editor.

"A human life is like a single letter in the alphabet. It can be meaningless. Or it can be part of a great meaning."

—National Planning Committee of Jewish Theological Seminary of America, 9/5/1956

Contents

Preface — iii
Acknowledgement — x
Introduction — xii

I Part I

"I'm all alone with no one to love me" — 3
"…a brain that's a pinin'" — 6
"I remember mighty well" — 17
"…we all lived happy together." — 23
"I keep right on with my conjure" — 30
"The folks keeps on comin' to be conjured" — 35
"…eight miles east of Coffeetown" — 43
"You know, I'm an "injun" — 49
"…out of my baby ways" — 55
"I got me a good man" — 62

II Part II

"My father's hut was enjoyed by all"	73
"My brothers and sisters are all dead"	80
"My father was a big man"	85
"…and soon they are dead"	90
"I'm coming to see you every day."	98
"Folks comes and helps me, but I'm tired now"	104
"Sit and 'bide."	110
"…to know them and their secret ways."	113
Pictures	137
Index	148
Notes	160
About the Author	185

Preface

On April 19, 1986, I left my home in Chattanooga, Tennessee, to drive 500 miles northeast to Quantico, Virginia. I was joining the FBI as a special agent. A recent graduate from Engineering school, I had applied to the FBI with no expectations. The FBI was never a dream job for me, and honestly, I had never really imagined myself living anywhere other than Chattanooga. I was born on Sand Mountain, in DeKalb County, Alabama, on the farm of my grandfather, Eldridge C. Thomas in 1962. Although my family later moved to the city of Chattanooga, where I grew up, Sand Mountain, or "The Mountain" as we called it, always remained "home" for my family.

Over the 25 years following my entry on duty, the FBI took me far from that home, both geographically and figuratively. During the first few months of my career—those spent at the training facility in Quantico, Virginia—I spent almost every weekend in a tottering old car making the long trip back to Chattanooga. I made most of those trips with another new agent/trainee named Michael Elliott. Mike was also from Tennessee and was also a newly-minted engineer. Special agent Merit Jenkins had recruited both of us simultaneously. Jenkins was also the one who introduced us. Jenkins told Mike to look me up when he arrived at Quantico and "hitch a ride home."

Mike was from Knoxville, about an hour and a half closer to Quantico than Chattanooga. Over the next 18 weekends, we spent about 16 hours on the road together each week.

We talked about almost everything a couple of college-age men could think to talk about during those long hours on the road. Mike was married, and I was engaged, so we covered women pretty quickly. We talked about family, friends, movies, our favorite TV show (The Andy Griffith Show, of course), music, favorite jokes, politics, religion, etc. One subject we heavily discussed was our deep and enduring curiosity for mysteries. Long portions of Interstate 81 would pass as we discussed real-world cases like John F. Kennedy's assassination, the D. B. Cooper hijacking, and many others. We also talked about paranormal encounters with Big Foot, UFOs, and ghosts.

It was during one of the many talks on ghosts when I shared the story of Granny Dollar. I first learned of Granny Dollar as a young boy when my cousin, Lanita, sketched out her life for me. She had written a biographical essay in school and chose the local legend and myth of Granny Dollar as her subject. At the time, unless you were from DeKalb County, it was unlikely that you would have heard of Granny Dollar. But as time went on, and with more efforts to uncover her story, her legend grew. Since I was from the city, I was not familiar with Granny Dollar. But, as my cousin gave her presentation, I became captivated by her story and wanted to know more. With little information available, I quickly learned that the small amount I knew of Granny Dollar was all that had been written up to that time and all that was known. Even as I turned my attention to other mysteries, I never could completely shake my fascination with Granny Dollar.

For 25 years following my arrival at Quantico, I continued to work as an FBI agent in addition to raising a family, traveling the world, and working on many interesting and challenging cases. Along the way, I became deeply interested and involved in genealogy. I spent many lunch hours in the National Archives and Library of Congress, in Washington, DC, "shagging leads" as they say in the FBI. After retiring, I moved back to the Chattanooga area to settle down. I then turned much of my idle time and attention to my research on genealogy and local history.

In 2017, Neil Wooten, a DeKalb County resident, wrote a novel called *Granny Dollar*. While I was reading that novel, my interest in the "mystery"" of Granny Dollar was rekindled. By the time I read Mr. Wooten's book, I was fortunate enough to have 25 years of law enforcement experience and a slew of genealogy research behind me. I was able to apply the skepticism and investigative skills developed in those years, to see flaws in the tale of Granny Dollar—flaws that I had not previously recognized. These flawed facts would lead to questions that would then lead me to the real identity of Granny Dollar. I was also able to make logical assessments about her character and motivations and to conclude that her true story was not what the tales suggested. This book documents the result of those pursuits.

This book is different from any previous works on Granny Dollar. It doesn't simply retell her tall tales. It isn't a "listen to what Granny says" book. It also isn't about me, or my career, or about the "hunt for the truth." This book is about the real woman who came to be called Granny Dollar and the context in which she emerged as a curiosity and local celebrity. It is also about some of the people who crossed her path and inhabited her life. It tells a poignant story of the impoverished life in Appalachia in the 1800s and early 1900s. It offers a first look at the real Granny Dollar who became the legend. I hope not to diminish that legend, but nourish it and grow it.

What prompted me to dig into the story of Granny Dollar? From the perspective of a 25-year veteran investigator, her story seemed flawed. Throughout the years, almost every writer who commented on Granny Dollar's tale expressed some level of doubt in the story. But, after finding little information about her—beyond her tale itself, each writer ultimately gave up digging deeper and acknowledged that "if the story was true", it was an extraordinary one. But, to a criminal investigator, such doubts induce more than curiosity and surrender. They call for inquiry and raise more questions—questions that have, until now, rarely been asked and never been answered.

Of course, I have benefitted from conditions that earlier writers did not have. I have access to genealogy information that, until recent years, wasn't readily available. Online census records, criminal records, newspaper archives, cemetery records, etc., have revolutionized the research process. No longer is a researcher obliged to trudge all over the map visiting libraries and county courthouses, interviewing surviving family members. Much of the information, once barely imaginable, is readily available with just a few clicks. I also benefited from the work of earlier researchers and writers on the subject. Each author has contributed in some substantial way to the story that is documented here.

Among the many responsibilities of the criminal investigator and prosecutor team is the responsibility of explaining to the jury the significance of evidence as it relates to proof. In pursuing, and then explaining the evidence, the investigator must construct a story that best fits the facts at hand. But, it is the jury who tries the facts, and it is the responsibility of the jury to determine whether the story reflects the truth "beyond a reasonable doubt." For the story of Granny Dollar, it will be the reader who will act as the jury to determine whether the explanations I present here rise to the level necessary to "prove" the case.

In seeking the truth, I have come to see Granny Dollar in a different light. To me, she has become much more than the character of an old Indian woman who scared children. She has become a real human being. She faced life's struggles with grit. She survived and made a name for herself in a time when that was not easy for a woman to do. Thus, I have developed a new respect for her. I hope that the reader will come to share those feelings of respect.

A note on style and structure:

To engage and satisfy the reader, I have tried to write in an entertaining style and have tried to avoid having too many quotes or references to records. I have included an extensive endnote section, where the reader will find references to documents and some explanations of what I was thinking when I wrote the main text. When writing biographical nonfiction, particularly about one so sparsely documented as Granny Dollar, it is necessary and common for the writer to extrapolate story details and make logical conclusions. In doing so, I have created a work that tracks, as closely as practical, to the truth without being a boring recitation of records and facts. In taking this license, I have shifted from the role of investigator to the role of entertainer.

Also, I have chosen to use a few words that may be considered archaic and, to some people, offensive. For example, Granny Dollar referred to herself as an "Indian" or "Injun." I have chosen to use the word "Indian" to refer to her purported ethnicity rather than with arguably less-offensive terms such as "Native American," "American Indian," or "Indigenous American." I recognize that the term "Indian" is often considered offensive when used by non-natives. Where the text supports it, I refer to the people as "Cherokee" or "Creek." I hope my usage of these, and similar, terms do not offend the reader or the native people to which it refers.

Since the story of Granny Dollar is a regional story, it has normally been told without much geographic (or other) context. I believe it is important that I not assume readers know about the topic. As a result, I included geographic and cultural descriptions to assist the reader in placing Granny Dollar within a real-world context. I have also taken time to expand on the places and the people in the Granny Dollar story, including the writers who shaped the story.

I hope these preface and disclaimers have been informative and helpful. In the back of this book, I have also included a section expanding on details that I felt were not appropriate, for stylistic reasons, for inclusion in the main body of the text. This section is presented in the format of "question and answer."

Disclaimer

I am not a historian. I am an investigator and, in the capacity of a writer, I am a biographer. I have taken some care to describe the historical context of the Granny Dollar story. But, this story is not intended as a comprehensive history of the region or the practices of the people described.

Acknowledgement

No one writes a nonfiction book alone:

Special acknowledgment:
I owe a great debt of gratitude to a number of researchers and writers, editors, and others who have preceded me. Although no one has previously succeeded in uncovering the real identity of Granny Dollar, each has, in their own way, contributed to the facts and conclusions presented here.

I am also deeply grateful to a number of people who inspired or supported my efforts.

Some of these people and groups are:

Sadie Shrader, schoolteacher, writer, Fort Payne, Alabama

Milford W. Howard, journalist, entrepreneur, DeKalb County, Alabama

Elizabeth Simmons Howard, DeKalb County native, historian, author, biographer, and genealogist.

Zora Shay Strayhorn, historian, and writer, Mentone, Alabama.

Ann Young, Librarian, DeKalb County, Alabama

The staff, writers, and editors of Landmarks of DeKalb County, Alabama

Will Dillard, journalist, Mentone, Alabama

Lanita Whitten Davidson, my cousin who first introduced me to the legend of Granny Dollar

Stacci Thomas, my sister and advisor, who first suggested that the Granny Dollar story was worth another look.

Neal Wooten, novelist, publisher, DeKalb County, Alabama.

Bill Potter, founder, and curator of the *DeKalb County, Alabama Historical Group*.

Introduction

The lens through which we view the world is murky. Our "reality" is strongly influenced by our beliefs and by the limited information to which we have exposure. In the character of Granny Dollar, we have limited information. In perceiving her story, we must deal with our modern beliefs as well as those of the many writers who have honored her tale. To really comprehend her story, we must understand the beliefs and superstitions shared within the context of her culture.

In the "old days," in the isolated mountains and hollows of Appalachia, people were self-reliant out of necessity. Dirt roads, where there were roads at all, weren't suitable for rapid travel. Communication between farms and communities moved only as fast as a horse and buggy would allow. Illiteracy, superstition, and a deep distrust of strangers added to the isolation. And in this isolation, there developed an ideology for explaining misfortune, such as the cause of storms and droughts, unexpected deaths, and financial losses.

When there was a medical need, there were few options. People had to rely on what they had and what they knew. Outsiders, even if trustworthy, were not readily available. Over the years, communities developed a culture of folk healing to address their medical needs. Folk healing, or "folk magic", was a mix of traditional practices, herbal medicine, the power of suggestion, and a dash of superstition. The knowledge to stop bleeding, set bones, and guide babies and mothers through difficult births, was priceless and guarded. Powers of observation, communication, patience, and other skills associated with health care work were only learned through practice. The ability to decide and then act, without fear, was an admirable trait. Thus, the character of the wise, old granny woman was developed. Granny women were part mystic, part conjurer, part prayer warrior, and part wise grandmother. They plied their craft throughout their communities, usually for free, and passed on their secrets to select learners through rituals, handing down the secret knowledge of their trade[1].

By the time Granny Dollar emerged from obscurity in 1923, the knowledge of granny women outside their rural communities was meager and scattered. As a result, outsiders did not recognize Granny Dollar for the character she was[2].

For almost a century, Granny Dollar has existed in the collective conscience of a northeast Alabama community as a folksy, homespun, hometown character. Her image prevailed as a rugged, gray-haired Cherokee woman, standing almost six-feet tall, clenching a corncob pipe in her teeth, and spinning yarns about history, conjuring, healing, and fortune-telling—**"Listen to what Grandma says!"**

Until now, Granny Dollar has existed as a caricature with certain characteristics and details of her life either exaggerated or omitted entirely from her story. In the end, this image was utilized by her neighbors and the few journalists who took note of her lore, to arouse curiosity to promote a distinctly-southern cultural identity.

Initially, the character of "Granny" was invented by Nancy Dollar herself but for completely different reasons. This book will peel back the persona that Nancy Dollar carefully constructed and protected to expose her true identity. It will also attempt to describe how she became the legend and character we know as "Granny Dollar." Lastly, this book will delve into her efforts to survive a backward culture to reveal a poignant tale of passion, betrayal, theft, and death.

Unfortunately, all those who knew Granny Dollar have long since passed away. All we have remaining are a few short written articles, some oral tales, and a handful of dispersed records. At the time that Granny Dollar lived, everyone accepted her identity for how she portrayed herself. Therefore, no one conducted any serious research or made much of an effort to dig deep into her past. In more recent times, there have been a few attempts to clarify the fog of her history, but without a starting point, name, birth date, or birthplace, and no family members to question, all efforts have fallen short. Almost every writer, who has taken on the subject of Granny Dollar, has expressed some level of doubt as to the veracity of her story. And yet, none have recognized the tales as anything but a near-faithful retelling of the truth.

Since she died in 1931, Granny Dollar has grown from a minor curiosity into a legend and almost a mythical figure. Today, a community celebrates her as a long-lived "Indian" midwife[3] and folk healer, a witch, and even a ghost (with a companion ghost-dog)[4]. She has been the subject of at least one novel,[5] a play,[6] and a one-woman monologue[7]. She appears as the subject of many blogs, Pinterest pages, and Youtube videos. And she has been discussed in several books about Southern ghosts and on Native Americans. Tourists can even travel to Mentone, Alabama, and rent a "Granny Dollar Holler Cabin." Both *the San Francisco Examiner* and the Federal Writers' Project of the Works Progress Administration have covered her[8]. Robert Ripley even wrote about Granny Dollar in his famed *Believe it or Not* book series.

So, who exactly was Granny Dollar? For her years alive, variously claimed to be 101 to 116 years, she left little in the way of records and documentation. Though she submitted to at least three interviews (two by professional columnists) in the roughly three years that she enjoyed as a minor celebrity, she divulged little verifiable information on her true identity. In the early 1970s, the *Landmarks of DeKalb County* rekindled interest in Granny Dollar. They began to gather information from a variety of sources, including people with a living memory of her, and put together a historical account[9]. But even that account lacked the key details needed to identify her as a real historical person rather than the persona she had become.

The tale of Granny Dollar prevails, in part, because it feeds our own persistent and secret desires. In 2014, the *Indian Country Today* newspaper wrote, "Everyone wants to be an Indian, but nobody wants to be an Indian." The statement is a paraphrase of a similar statement made by comedian Paul Mooney. Mooney meant that people from other cultures like to adopt choice pieces from a minority culture, but don't really want to live as a part of that culture. Whether these bits and pieces provide a quick path to spirituality, or feed into a particular fantasy someone may have, people desire connection with certain aspects of Indian culture. For some, the legend of Granny Dollar creates a proxy connection to Native culture with a bonus hope that we, too, can live to a ripe old age.

This book will not only retell the story Granny Dollar nurtured about herself, but it will also document her rise to legendary status after 1923. But, it won't stop there. It will identify the historical person who became Granny Dollar and will document her birth, her age, her spouse, and immediate family members as well as many of the circumstances of her life and the lives of those around her. The reader will learn that Granny Dollar's tale about her own life was a myth that she constructed over many years to help her achieve economic autonomy by laboring as a granny midwife, folk healer and conjurer[10]. This tale she spun was also useful to her by covering some shameful details surrounding her family's history. Ultimately, her persona served to ensure her well-being and security when she could no longer work and in a place and time when a single woman had few alternatives.

In 2014, the Mentone area newsletter *The Groundhog* published a series of six articles documenting Granny Dollar's story and her life from 1923 until a little after her death. But, until now, all factual stories about Granny Dollar have been a retelling of her story she "wrote" about herself. Neal Wooten, who wrote the 2017 novel, *Granny Dollar*[11], conducted substantial research and concluded that Granny's story, over 85 years after her death, could only be told in a fictional novel. Wooten writes that "until someone does even more hard work to discover the obscure sources that could authenticate the Granny Dollar story," his historical fiction novel would "remain the closest we have to her biography."

This book is the result of the hard work he describes. It will present a new story, sewn together by facts and reconciled with her claims, along with reasonable conclusions drawn from these sources and stories. It will add color, not only to Granny Dollar, but to the many people who occupied her world—people who, until now, have been unknown, or simply names in a story.

But as this is not a perfect work on Granny Dollar, it will just be one of many more to come as further areas of research are undertaken. Also, some may disagree with many of the conclusions I have drawn. Nevertheless, I hope this book will add to the knowledge we have on Granny Dollar, and shed light on who she was and why we should care.

I

Part I

"Notoriety wasn't as good as fame, but was heaps better than obscurity."
— Neil Gaiman, Good Omens: The Nice and Accurate Prophecies of Agnes Nutter, Witch

"I'm all alone with no one to love me"

It was in the early fall of 1923[12] when "Granny," in her "Mother Hubbard" dress,[13] appeared suddenly on the doorstep of the Master School four miles south of Mentone. In one hand, she carried a sack containing all her worldly possessions, and in the other, she clutched a corncob pipe "ready for use". Her vicious[14] 12-year-old dog, "Buster" hovered protectively nearby. She was poor and alone, since the death of her husband barely five months earlier, and unable to care for herself. She feared going to the poorhouse[15] or, worse, resorting to suicide. Having walked nearly 10 miles to get there, she looked exhausted and much older than her 75 years[16].

When the boys and girls of the mountain boarding school first saw Granny, they couldn't help but think that a witch[17] had walked out of the woods. Her name was Nancy Dollar[18], but she was known in the community as "Grandma" or "Granny." The children gathered around her in curiosity. She talked funny and smelled of sour snuff[19] and cheap pipe tobacco. Her frame was massive, her hands were calloused from years of farm work, and her face showed the wisdom of her age in its lines. Her way of speaking was abrupt, and her voice hoarse and deep[20]. Even the words she used were strange, but the strangest thing about the way she talked was her directness. Granny didn't hesitate to say what she needed and what she wanted[21].

The weather in the summer of 1923 had been unusually cool on the mountain. Cotton and gardens were doing fine, and mosquitoes were not a big problem. But, signs pointed to early, and colder-than-usual, winter. People were even predicting snow, which was a rare thing in the Alabama mountains. And Granny was one who watched the signs of weather[22].

The mountain schoolchildren of the Master School eagerly sought approval from their Dean, to lodge Granny in an old cabin that sat empty on the school grounds. They would then wait for the school's founder and benefactor, Colonel Milford Wriarson Howard, to return from visiting with his wife in California, to figure out what to do with Granny.

In the meantime, the boys couldn't get enough of Granny. She took advantage of the opportunity to settle herself, Buster, and their things in the old, two-room cabin. From an old broken-down chair on the porch, she could watch the children doing the chores she now struggled to do herself, such as drawing water, hauling firewood, and kindling fires. Boys rushed in and out with other supplies too, like tobacco for her iconic corncob pipe and the fixings for Granny's soup pot. From the cabin's porch, Granny held court while dozens of eager ears listened as she spun yarns about Indians, wars, feuds, and killing.[23]

Granny Dollar continued to live in the little two-room cabin near Colonel Howard for the remaining seven and one-half years of her life. Even as the Master School shut down and much of the property passed into the possession of new owners, she continued to "rent" the cabin from Howard. During this time, Granny entertained many school children and later camp children, neighbors, journalists, politicians, and summer visitors. Her reputation as a fortune-teller, folk healer, gardener, and storyteller continued to flourish. When she died in 1931, she was mourned by a vast community, and her death was reported by dozens of newspapers throughout the state.

In the years following her death, her story became campfire fodder for the dozens of camps for boys and girls that saturated the Lookout Mountain wilderness. The youth in these summer camps, after a day immersed in nature, would gather around campfires to sing and share stories of legends and ghosts.

Along with common tales of *the Monkey's Paw, the Green Hand, the Hook-Handed Killer,* and *the Legend of Three-Fingered Willie,* tales of Granny Dollar's ghost emerged. By early 1961—and surely far earlier—stories of Granny's ghost, and that of Buster's ghost too, were circulating widely. Dozens of stories of Granny having money or treasure buried near her home emerged in the years following her death. It was said that she could be seen, particularly around the anniversary of her death, near her cabin, accompanied, as always, by her ghost-dog Buster as they search for her lost "Indian" gold.

"...a brain that's a pinin'"

When Granny first made her appearance, the Master School for Southern Mountain Boys and Girls on Lookout Mountain was brand new, having been dedicated on Sunday, September 2, 1923. The governor of Alabama gave a special address, and the town enjoyed a spectacular fireworks display and "dinner on the grounds." A large flag was unfurled above the school building as an enthusiastic sign of the school's Americanism. The school was the vision, passion, and achievement of Colonel Howard, who was quite the offbeat character himself. He led several creative, but chiefly failed, projects in northeast Alabama during the early 1900s. Among these, beginning in 1923, was the Master School. This school was the first, and only, of a series of schools envisioned to support underprivileged children in the rural mountain communities of Appalachia[24].

City people had always been fascinated by the southern mountains. Economic conditions were unsatisfactory and social services, including education, were inadequate. It was believed that these conditions, symptoms of the isolation prevalent in the mountains, set the people of these areas back when compared to other 'normal' farming communities. These sentiments often led to hackneyed misrepresentations about the people of this region. But while the reality of life in the mountains was often exaggerated, school conditions in the early 1900s were a real and difficult problem. And to add to this problem, governments were, for many reasons, slow to undertake policies to rehabilitate these areas.

In much of the farming south, schools started after the harvest and ended before the planting season. But, in the mountain communities where large crop farming was rare[25], children were responsible for more than just helping out in the planting and harvesting of row crops. Mountain children were relied upon to help hunt, fish, kill and dress livestock, smoke meat, spin and weave cloth, sew clothes, make rope and bedding, cut and split wood, draw and carry water, churn butter, make soap, collect honey, drive and feed livestock, milk cows, train horses and mules, and even occasionally tend the stills, among many other laborious tasks. This substantial amount of work expected from the youth of Appalachia meant that 'schoolin'' often took a back seat.

In the early 1900s, school busses were uncommon on the rugged and narrow mountain roads. As a result, most mountain children were obliged to walk to school. So to give the communities a chance at education, this meant that schools had to be plentiful. One-room schools often popped up on donated lands in virtually every community, the costs of constructing and maintaining these buildings falling on the residents themselves.

Although most of the parents in these communities were uneducated and illiterate, many recognized the value of education and inherently felt that times were changing. They knew that to provide the best for their children; they needed to educate them. Unfortunately, few families could afford to lose the labor of their children while still paying for their education. The solution? The creation of working schools where children could contribute to and reduce the operating expenses and costs of their education.

In DeKalb County, Alabama in 1923, schools of two classes, city schools and rural schools, were administered by a County Board of Education. Teachers were paid under 1-year independent contracts, with most supplies being provided by the local communities. In rural districts, including Lookout Mountain, residents were required to maintain an average attendance of at least 10 students to justify the cost of a teacher. In October, in the valley below Lookout Mountain, the high school opening would wait, as usual, until the cotton was out of the fields in the middle of the month, but The Fort Payne City Grammar School had opened its doors in the first week of September. All grammar school-age children living within the city limits of Fort Payne, about 500 in all, were required to attend the public school. But, seven miles above Fort Payne on the summit of Lookout Mountain, the 'mountain kids', many of whom had been unschooled, would start their first school term at the brand new Master School.

Howard, who had a soft spot for the Appalachian "mountaineers," was living in California in the early 1920s. He dreamed of returning to Lookout Mountain to start a school for poor mountain children, following Berry College's founder

Martha Berry's successful model. His vision was an outgrowth of his first novel, *Peggy Ware*[26]. In the book, the title character built a school for impoverished children in Buck's Pocket, a canyon in nearby Sand Mountain. Many, if not most, of the adults that lived in the surrounding rural areas of Lookout Mountain to the east, and Sand Mountain to the west, were semi-literate. Their children, required to work on the small farms and in the coal mines and lumber and sawmill enterprises of their families, were following in their parents' footsteps.

Colonel Howard longed to repair this injustice, beginning with the Master School. Howard believed in the ingenuity of the hearty Scots-Irish frontiersmen that had settled primarily in the Appalachian mountains' backcountry. He firmly believed that, if given a chance at an education, these mountaineers would prosper in ways that would exceed those of the valley-dwellers. He also thought that the Master School would be the first of other similar schools making the difference.

By 1923, Howard was in Hollywood, writing and making motion pictures while his wife, Sally, successfully speculated in real estate. In the spring of that year, Howard's cousin, Vivian Stella (Lloyd) Harper, wrote to him in California from Brunswick, Georgia. In the letter, she told him that she had read his book *Peggy Ware*, and had experienced a vision in which she saw exactly where and how he would accomplish the first school building. She also dedicated herself to helping him accomplish that dream. Howard was thrilled. Leaving Sally in California, he returned to Lookout Mountain to undertake what his brainchild, Peggy Ware, had accomplished in fiction.

After boarding a train in Los Angeles on June 18, Howard arrived in Fort Payne on June 23. There, he met Vivian. The two immediately headed to Buck's Pocket in search of a suitable site for the school, and to scout out a filming location for the movie based on his novel.[27] Finding no suitable land for sale, Howard, who had only $100 to his name at the time, returned to Fort Payne disappointed. The next day, he and Vivian headed for Lookout Mountain and soon found themselves standing on the future site of the Master School. Howard rushed back to Fort Payne and borrowed the money to purchase 750 acres[28] from The Alabama State Land Company.

Construction on the school began July 22, 1923 with workers spending much of the remaining summer constructing a five-mile dirt road to a clearing of several acres designated for construction. Plans were drawn up for a substantial school building, a couple of dormitories, and numerous workshops. The buildings were to be constructed in units, so they could be added to as needed. On Lookout Mountain's "Little Mountain," they built a 24' x 34' schoolhouse of native stone topped by pine shingles, two 18' x 52' frame dormitories, and a 16' x 26' dining hall. With construction ongoing, the school opening was planned for September, a mere three months after Howard's return to Alabama. Nearby, Howard constructed a cabin of his own.

When Granny Dollar arrived in the fall of 1923, the Master School was already as impoverished as the community it was envisioned to serve. Although no one knew at the time, the school, which was less than two months old, was already on its last legs. Howard's wife continued to send money from California, and Howard himself would undertake several efforts locally to obtain operating funds to keep the school alive. This included selling off lots on the remainder of the property and soliciting donations from the community[29].

In July 1923, the people of Fort Payne had generously donated over $1,600 out of their pockets after an impromptu request by Howard. But, expected donations from outside the local community would not appear[30]. By November 1923, teachers from the school traveled to Birmingham to beg librarians for their discarded children's books. Howard would even host the governor of Alabama in a Fourth of July bash at the school in an attempt to raise funds. In 1924, Howard hosted a "big bench show" and fox hunt at Wade's Gap and raffled off two building lots. But, all efforts would prove to be insufficient.[31] When Granny Dollar arrived, Howard was already struggling to fund continued construction on the school. He struggled to feed the 40 to 50 boys and girls who lived at the school, as well as pay the salaries of three teachers, a dean, and a handyman.[32]

So, it was with great hesitation that he allowed Granny's presence at the school to continue. She had arrived while Howard was away visiting Sally in California. His cousin Vivian, who had become the dean and "fore lady" of the school, had approved her presence "in the enthusiasm of the moment." For his own part, Howard had been thinking about organizing a department for adult illiterates, many of them far past the meridian of life. He wanted to teach them to read and write and instill into their minds the great fundamental principles on which he had founded his school. Perhaps, he thought, Granny Dollar could be his first adult student. But, another mouth to feed was almost too much despite his soft spot for mountaineers.

The schoolboys continued treating Granny like a queen by cutting firewood, making fires, and carrying water on her behalf. Howard just couldn't bear to break it up. He was also intimidated by Granny and could not find it in himself to throw a supposedly 100-year-old woman out of her cabin. After all, she had nowhere else to go. After Howard returned to Alabama, despite his money woes, he acquiesced, agreeing that if everyone else starved, Granny might as well starve along with them. However, Howard hoped that if he didn't explicitly approve of Granny's presence or welcome her overtly, she might move on. So, he tried to avoid all contact with her[33].

Before their meeting, Nancy Dollar had intentionally sought out Howard[34]. He was remarkably prominent in the area and known as a supporter of the indigent—especially children—of the mountain. He was a big promoter of the mountaineer and had often noted about how, while the people of Appalachia had done much for their country, they received little in return[35].

Journalists had prominently written about the Master School project in the Fort Payne newspaper all summer. The people of the mountain were talking about it too, and dozens had found jobs working on the school's construction. Forty to fifty children had been accepted, and many more had registered. But, due to a lack of space and resources, many were not accepted. The talk was that the project would offer children a chance to work for their keep and education by tending gardens and orchards, raising chickens, and participating in other farming-related activities[36].

Granny Dollar was aware of the school's talk[37] and the presence of construction crews all summer. Even though the school was on shaky financial ground, she could not have found a better situation or picked a better benefactor on all of Lookout Mountain.

Although they were not yet acquainted[38], Howard had probably heard of Nancy Dollar too. Although he was living in California[39] before returning to build the Master School, he had spent many years in northern Alabama. Granny had lived there for over 25 years at that point. She and her husband had moved often, renting farm to farm, including occasional moves across the Alabama border into neighboring Walker County, Georgia. But, Nelson Dollar had served for several years as an election officer for Beat 12 in DeKalb County, and the region was sparsely populated. The Dollars had formerly lived near Cloudmont[40], about four miles north of the Master School on the road to Mentone. Before 1919, they lived at the Tutwiler place, close to the school site. Additionally, Nelson Dollar and Milford Howard both had kin living in nearby Rome, Georgia, so they may have been familiar with each other's families.

Granny Dollar herself was not unknown. Residents and tourists would often stop by to have their fortunes told and to bring her food. In her later years, during the warmer months, she had visitors almost every day. She was also active and known within her community as a folk healer and a midwife. It is from these pursuits that she acquired her nickname[41], "Granny." While it is clear that they were on different social strata, and were not formally acquainted, Howard and Granny Dollar were undoubtedly aware of each other.

Milford Howard was born in 1862, near Rome, Georgia; he was the first of six children. At the age of five, his family moved to Randolph County, Arkansas, where they lived in wretched poverty. By the age of 11, Howard was producing two-horse crops with his nine-year-old brother, and, at age 12, he was working at a cotton gin for 30 cents a day. As a result, he received less than a year of formal education. After returning to Georgia in 1876, Howard pursued the study of law under Joseph A. Blanche, an attorney in Cedartown, Georgia, after pestering him enough to impress him. By the time he was 19, he had been admitted into the Georgia bar. After Howard's father passed through Fort Payne, Alabama, on a work trip, he recommended the town to his son as a good place to make a living. On November 7, 1881, without knowing a single soul in the town, Howard arrived in Fort Payne to begin a law career—taking with him the honorary title of "Colonel."[42] Similar to Granny Dollar, when she showed up on the doorstep of the Master School, Howard arrived in Fort Payne wearing the only full set of clothes he owned and carrying a little bundle of shirts and underwear, a comb and brush, a Bible, and thirty dollars.

After passing the Alabama bar and building a successful practice in Fort Payne, Howard decided to run for political office. Despite being vigorously opposed by almost every Alabama politician of the day (even those of his own party), Howard was elected. He served two terms in Washington, DC representing the people of Alabama in the House of

Representatives. But, Howard quickly grew disillusioned by Washington, and, declining to run for a third term, he returned to Alabama to practice law. He made and lost two separate fortunes investing, first in Mexican mining and then in a Louisiana oil field. Each time, he would return to the practice of law to build up his fortune again. After yet another failed investment in an Alaskan salmon cannery, Howard left Alabama to spend several years living in California, working as a writer, an actor, and a movie-maker. He published three moderately successful books, including a fiction novel. In 1918, after losing more money, he returned, yet again, to Alabama to dedicate himself to his various projects for the improvement of the people of Alabama. He then returned to California to resume his movie-making while Sally embarked on a somewhat successful career as a real estate speculator. Howard left her in California when he returned to Lookout Mountain in 1923 to build the Master School with his cousin Vivian. He and his wife would never live together again.

Although Howard proved to have a sharp intellect, powerful vision, and good instincts, he had no understanding of finances and little practicality. He never lacked enthusiasm and fearlessly launched projects with initial success, only to fail again and again. He could rally the public, manipulate the press, and generally start anything he chose to start. But he could not finish. The Master School would be another one of his failures. By 1925, a mere two years after he chartered it, Howard had sold the school and moved on to a plan to build a broad boulevard along the top of Lookout Mountain from Gadsden, Alabama, to Chattanooga, Tennessee. Even though the Master School was a failed project and was quickly left behind, Granny was not left alone. She continued to live in Howard's spare cabin at River Park, and he continued to provide her with the basics of life. She became a sort of mascot for the boys' camp there, and there was little else to distinguish her life before coming to the school from her life after arriving there. She continued to raise vegetables, fruit, and chickens, always having plenty to give away or barter with the local peddler or neighbors in exchange for things she could not make or grow. She occasionally told fortunes to earn what little cash she could and was probably still called upon to sit with the sick, cure a wart or a wen (cyst), or nurse the flu. She continued to identify locations for digging to find a sure-fire Indian treasure and probably spent a good bit of time digging herself. She also remained a source of entertainment for the boys and girls camps at DeSoto Falls. Howard introduced her to almost every visitor, representing that Granny was an "authentic" mountaineer. Newspapers took little notice. From 1923 until the end of 1928, she was just another poor, elderly resident of Lookout Mountain in DeKalb County, Alabama.

"I remember mighty well"

So, how did Nancy Dollar go from being a local oddity and favorite teller of tales to a legend? On January 28, 1928, *The Progressive Farmer and Farm Woman*[43] magazine published the first important article about Granny Dollar. The article, *An Indian Daughter of the Confederacy, Listen to What "Grandma" Dollar Says at the Age of 101 Years*, recorded many of the "memories" of Nancy Callahan[44] Dollar. The writer was not a professional journalist, but a New Oregon[45], Alabama school teacher named Sadie Shrader. New Oregon was a small community on Lookout Mountain just above the valley town of Fort Payne. The Shraders, Sadie and her husband Erskine, moved to New Oregon in late 1925. By 1927, Sadie was teaching at nearby Rock Bridge School[46] and Erskine was working at Cloudland[47]. Her article was only a couple of pages long and included a few photographs and a drawing[48]. Yet, it is from this article that much of what we know about Granny Dollar came to light.

Sadie was the oldest child of William Brownly McCurdy and Julia Adeline Reese. The McCurdy family was one of the oldest white families to settle in DeKalb County. They arrived there, around 1836, from Lincoln County, Tennessee (via Jackson County, Alabama)[49]. The McCurdy's eventually moved from the valley settlement of Lebanon west to Sand Mountain and Brownly McCurdy became a very successful farmer. His children attended school and were well-educated. Sadie attended high school in the valley school at Fort Payne, graduating formally, along with her brother Garfield and six other students, in 1914 when she was 26 years old[50]. She also attended teacher training school at Chavies[51]. Later, she taught at Mahan School near Sylvania, Alabama, then her own school, seven miles west of Valley Head in a community called Jude[52]

The family of Erkine Shrader was also an early Sand Mountain family. They settled at Pisgah on the border of DeKalb County and neighboring Jackson County, in early 1850. The Shraders were farmers, but Erskine Shrader's father, John Charles Shrader, was also operating a moonshine distillery, along with his brother George, near Rosalie as early as 1897. Erskine lived, for much of his childhood, with his grandfather, Daniel Shrader, while his father was away in federal prison, paying for his criminal enterprise. In March 1913, after a brief move to Fort Payne, the Shrader family moved to Jude and settled near the McCurdy family. Sadie and Erskine married a little over a year later on June 4, 1914. She was 26 years old, and he was 21.

When Sadie and her husband Erskine moved to Lookout Mountain, Sadie's brother, Phillip Garfield McCurdy, moved there as well to teach at the Master School[53] where Granny was living. At the time the Shraders arrived, Granny Dollar was recovering from a recent ankle injury from a fall. Many people from the local community were regularly looking in on her, caring for her in the way that she had cared for her community for decades. While it's possible the Shraders knew about Granny Dollar before their arrival, they became well acquainted immediately when Sadie moved to the area.

Granny Dollar, though poor, was generous. She was careful to cultivate friends by giving away vegetables from her garden, fruit from her orchards, and extra eggs from her "Indian" chickens. As a midwife and folk healer,[54] she was in the business of knowing her neighbors and meeting their needs. Sadie Shrader visited her often and benefited from Granny's garden and her folk wisdom.

On one such visit, in June of 1927[55], after listening to Granny spin yarns and prompting her to provide more details, Shrader carefully took notes and drew diagrams. She wrote a letter describing "Grandma Dollar" and submitted it, along with her drawings and photographs, to *The Progressive Farmer* magazine.

In the article, Shrader stated that Granny Dollar's name was Nancy Callahan Dollar, and she was called "Granny" or "Grandma." She was 101[56] at the time of the interview. She recalled the early days of her childhood well. Born on Sand Mountain, eight miles east of Coffeetown[57], Nancy claimed she was the daughter of a Cherokee father named William Callahan and a half-Cherokee and a half-Irish mother named Mary Sexton. In childhood, she enjoyed the games played by Indian children, including "dog and fox" and pitching quoits. She never attended school.

According to Granny, her father hunted wild game while the

rest of the family raised corn and potatoes. He also secretly had a second wife, named Cassie, and three other children in South Carolina[58]. Nancy's mother eventually allowed her husband to bring his second family to Alabama where they all lived together in a combined, communal family—an arrangement, she said, that the Cherokee permitted.

The two women labored happily together in raising the crops and caring for the family. Together, according to Granny, the two mothers produced a total of 26 children, including three sets of triplets born to Nancy's mother. The large family ate wild turkey, deer, and fish with vegetables, like cabbage, pumpkin, hominy, and corn, which was roasted "with the shuck on", in a red clay oven. Johnnie cake, sweetened with molasses, was also a special treat.

When most Native Americans were forcibly evicted from the area, William Callahan avoided moving his family from their home by hiding in a "saltpeter cave."[59] Later, however, he eventually left Alabama after an altercation with a white man named Jukes, whom Callahan had accused of murder. Fearing that the Jukes family might retaliate, Callahan moved his large family to Georgia and settled about 30 miles from Marthasville.[60]

According to the story, when Nancy was about 21 years old, one of the mothers died. To support her many younger brothers and sisters, Nancy sought a way to make money, so she could buy food. She began hauling goods from the village of Marthasville to the country stores near her home, a distance of 30 miles. She hauled goods such as molasses, meat, salt, powder, lead, gun caps, shoes, dishes, and wagon tires from Kyle Brothers Wholesalers for 15 or 20 years. During this period she became engaged to a storekeeper's son named Thomas Porter. Tragically, however, Thomas died while fighting for the Confederate Army in the Civil War. Nancy remained single for over 40 years after his death.

The war brought more tragedy to the "Callahan" family. When the Union forces first reached Atlanta, William Callahan sent his daughter word not to go into Atlanta for more goods, but to stay home with the children. From 30 miles away, Nancy said, she heard the roar of the cannon. Nancy's father did not survive the battle. Nancy was forced to assume full responsibility for providing food for her siblings. Added to this burden, Nancy took in a neighbor woman named Madge Cole, along with her five children, after her husband had also been killed in the war. Together, they tended a small garden to help the three families, living as one, to survive.

After many years, Nancy returned to Alabama with her husband Nelson Dollar. For the next thirty years, she struggled to make a living on Lookout Mountain as a midwife[61] and folk healer. She also became somewhat of a regular character among the summer visitors of the nearby town of Mentone, by telling fortunes[62] and reading signs. She raised fruit, vegetables, and chickens to supplement her meager income, and Nelson Dollar had, for a short time, received a small pension.

After Nelson died, with no family to rely on for support in her aging years, Nancy did what anyone else would have done—she sought the support of neighbors. In the fall of 1923, Granny Dollar showed up on the doorstep of Colonel Howard's Master School[63]. She told her interviewer, "my brothers and sisters are all dead." Three years to the day from the publication date of *The Progressive Farmer* article about Granny Dollar, the January 28, 1931 issue of *The Fort Payne Journal* announced Nancy's death.

There is no indication that the Sadie Shrader article made much of an immediate impact or that anyone in the local area even took notice. This article became the core of the Granny Dollar story, but at the time, local newspapers were not interested in following it[64]. But, eventually, others did take notice, and Granny Dollar soon came to be viewed as a remarkable character in DeKalb County.

"...we all lived happy together."

It is helpful to understand the geography of the area where Granny Dollar lived. DeKalb County lies in the extreme northeastern corner of Alabama in the "ridge and valley" region of the Cumberland Plateau[65]. The county runs diagonally for roughly 50 miles from the northeast near Trenton, Georgia, ending just northeast of Albertville, Alabama.

Wills Valley is a narrow limestone valley stretching the length of the county[66]. The valley runs along Big Wills Creek to its source at Valley Head and along Lookout Creek northeastward to the Georgia state line. The towns of Crossville, Fort Payne, and Valley Head are spread out, south-to-north, along Wills Valley. Fort Payne, one of the most substantial towns in DeKalb County, is the county seat. The valley is flanked on both sides by broad plateaus or table mountains. On the southwest side of DeKalb, and running its entire length, is Sand Mountain—a broad sandstone plateau lying about 900 feet above the valley floor. Along the southeast border of DeKalb, is its slightly higher, slightly more narrow twin, Lookout Mountain.

Although the entire area was extensively settled by the Creek and Cherokee peoples, early white settlers in DeKalb County initially established homesteads in the valley around 1820. In time, many settled in the surrounding mountains to take advantage of good farmland and slightly cooler summers. By 1840, large numbers of hearty pioneers were scattered all over Sand Mountain and Lookout Mountain. In 1852, the Wills Valley Railroad received its charter. By January 1862, construction of that line was completed as far west as Trenton, Georgia, and as far south as Gadsden, Alabama, by March 1863. Fueled by the requirements of the Civil War, the line grew quickly. It fed the fertile products of Wills Valley and the mountains into Chattanooga, Tennessee, simplifying the efforts of farmers and stockmen to get their crops and stock there.

The economy of the valley and the two mountains differ substantially. Sand Mountain is an open, flat plateau and its rich, well-drained loam is suitable for open crop farming. Sand Mountain has produced many crops over the years to include cotton, corn, soybeans, and potatoes. It was also known, in the late 1800s, for its cattle industry and later for its poultry. On the other hand, in the early 1900s, Lookout Mountain was less settled and open crop farming was less common. Family subsistence farms and grist mills dominated.

On Lookout Mountain, and on the northern end of Sand Mountain in the "Big Woods" area, a thriving timber industry existed. Standing timber was cut for firewood, sawlogs, fence posts, veneer logs, pulpwood, pilings, and poles. Mining and millwork were also common occupations on Lookout Mountain. From around 1880, Lookout Mountain, unlike its twin, had a thriving tourist business as wealthier citizens from all over the Southeastern United States flocked to the resorts scattered along the top of Lookout Mountain. On the northern end, at the brow overlooking Saint Elmo, Tennessee, the Lookout Inn welcomed visitors beginning in 1890. Later, in the 1920s, the Lookout Hotel opened on the Georgia side of the mountain. Farther south, at Mentone, an inn began to cater to tourists as early as the 1880s.

Sand Mountain and Lookout Mountain are both separated from the valley by a scarp face, which is a steep slope, or cliff, formed by erosion. The scarps abruptly separate the level valley floor from the level mountain tops. From Fort Payne, a narrow and steep, washboard dirt road switched back through Chavies and Davis Gaps, northwest of the town, up Sand Mountain to the settlement of Chavies. As late as the 1890s, the people of Sand Mountain were begging for "a better road or a flying machine!"

Similarly, on the Lookout Mountain side of the valley southeast of the town, an equivalent, but even steeper road, snaked up Beeson's Gap to the top of Lookout Mountain. This stretch of dirt road didn't receive chert gravel until 1921. *The Huntsville Times* humorously reported that it was a criminal act to route tourists from Scottsboro, in Paint Rock Valley to Mentone via this stretch of road. A trip up and down Sand Mountain, across the Big Wills Valley and up Lookout Mountain to Mentone, which today takes 45 minutes, took four-and-a-half hours in 1923.

About 10 miles northeast of Fort Payne, in Wills Valley, was the community of Valley Head. From Valley Head, going east, a traveler would climb through Tutwiler Gap about two miles to the top of Lookout Mountain. Passing numerous cottages and summer homes, the road joined Mentone Road, and headed toward DeSoto Falls and the DeSoto caves (or rock houses). On the right side of the road was "Idyllspot," the summer home of the Tutwiler family[67], and "Sky Hook," belonging to pilot Sumter Smith[68]. These houses had Brow Road on one side and the brow of Lookout Mountain, with its breath-taking view, on the other.

Continuing south, the road turned left at the top of Wade Gap and dropped into the river bottom area of Alpine Park. The campus of the Master School was here. Also, on the right of the road, was Sentinel Rock, the high flat boulder from which it was possible to look into four counties. On the left side of the road was the Master School and, on a huge boulder, a little log cabin built students to be a home of Colonel Howard.

A short distance away was the old cabin of "Granny Dollar." Then, the traveler would pass Alpine Lodge, a little picturesque Swiss chalet hanging over the roaring waters of Little River. All along the stream were cottages of natural rock and logs including Winward Inn, the cottage studio of Birmingham artist Clara Moorman. Further up was the DeSoto River (or West Fork Little River) where a modern bridge road was constructed in 1927 to connect to Lahoosage, Alabama. From Lahoosage, one could drive north a few miles to join Menlo Road (or the Dixie Highway), turn left, and arrive in Mentone.

The Little River is a rare mountaintop river. Most of its

length meanders down the middle of Lookout Mountain. From Cloudmont, in northwest Georgia, the river flows south through Little River Canyon (Mays Gulf) and joins the Coosa River near Centre, Alabama. In the 1890s and early 1900s, the area between the summer resort town of Mentone and Walker's Chapel was a parklike wilderness threaded by the Little River, its canyons and caves, and, until the late 1920s, an ancient chert road. From the 1890s through the beginning of the great depression, this area hosted a curious mixture of people. Locals mostly tended to small farms, cut timber, or mined coal. Many produced bootleg whisky[69] in the hollows and canyons of Lookout Mountain, and a steady stream of automobiles hauled it to illicit markets in Chattanooga along the Chattanooga-Birmingham Highway. Sawmills and grist mills dotted the landscape, along with churches of various denominations.[70] Numerous scout camps and youth summer camps existed among the forests of Little River. Several "fresh air" tuberculosis camps gave relief to suffering Alabamans. Dozens of waterfalls, springs, and rock formations awaited hundreds of backwoods campers, hikers, and horseback riders escaping the valley's heat.[71] In the mid-1920s, many locals toiled for free to clear stumps and grade and construct ditches to support modern roads in order to bring money-paying tourists into the region.[72]

In the 1880s, Frank Caldwell built a Victorian-style inn among the mineral springs of Mentone. By the 1920s, the business was booming as the heat-escaping city-dwellers flocked to the mountain to experience nature. By this time, Mentone had three stores, The Mentone Store, Charley Hall's, and J. N. Powell's. It also boasted two garages, four filling stations, four churches, and a school. It was a busy little mountain village. During this boom time, Caldwell's Inn offered swimming, fishing, tennis, bowling, croquet, billiards, box golf, and dancing for guests. They also had access to the two springs on the grounds, Mineral Springs and Beauty Springs. By 1924, a dam at DeSoto Falls was producing electricity for the resorts at Mentone and the factories and factory workers in Fort Payne. Beautifully-gowned ladies promenaded through rock gardens in Mentone while locals toiled on rented farms under crop-share contracts and busted stumps on the dirt roads leading to and from Mentone.[73] Visitors occasionally purchased moonshine from locals, and many hundreds had their fortunes told by Granny Dollar for a few cents[74].

The contrast between the haves and have-nots was evident in the valley too. Fort Payne had a boom of its own with the discovery of iron and coal deposits in the area. With both the Mentone boom and the Fort Payne boom, the area experienced explosive growth in economic activity and population. During this time, an influx of "Yankee" investors swelled the population to thousands. In Fort Payne, a 125-room hotel, occupying an entire city block, was constructed, and an Opera House was built in 1889 to help accommodate the growing cosmopolitan population. After the iron deposits played out, in 1907, W. B. Davis Hosiery Mill began operation. This was the beginning of decades of successful hosiery manufacturing in Fort Payne. Although it was small, Fort Payne was a thriving, modern town. Here, too, the distinction between rich and poor was noteworthy, but, among DeKalb residents, it was the distinction between the valley "rich" and the mountain "poor" that was most striking.[75] It was in this environment in the early 1920s, among the poor farming community of Lookout Mountain, that Granny Dollar first emerged.

"I keep right on with my conjure"

After Sadie Shrader's article appeared in *The Progressive Farmer* in January 1928, one would have expected that there would be follow-up articles in the local press. *The Fort Payne Journal*, however, did not cover the Granny Dollar story. The next mention of Granny in the local paper was to announce, in March 1929, that she was very ill and her recovery was doubtful. In January 1931, her death was announced.

By the end of summer in 1928, Milford Howard had mentioned Granny Dollar in his weekly news column only sparsely. [76] In June 1928, Winifred Black[77], of William Randolph Hearst's *San Francisco Examiner*, traveled to Mentone to visit Howard at his Alpine Lodge.[78] Her goal was to collect stories for her column under the theme of "My Country Tis of Thee."[79] Howard later wrote, "I began to see the glimmer of light in the darkness when she spoke of the "sort of people who make up America." Black had been sent to see Howard specifically so that he could tell her about the "Anglo Saxon Mountaineers."Howard said that "at that moment, a great light burst upon me." Black had hit upon his soft spot. He told Black, "Here is your story.[80]"

Winifred Black had a reputation as a "sob sister," which is a female journalist who writes articles with an overly sentimental appeal. She spent a weekend at the Alpine Lodge with Howard showing her the wonders of his mountains. According to Howard, she found "a new world here, refreshing her in body and spirit and [she] was thrilled by the simple things that appeal to great souls only." Among those simple things were swimming in the "pot hole[81]" in the DeSoto River and having her fortune told by Granny Dollar.

Granny told Black that she could sense a bit of "Indian" blood in Black herself. Granny, according to Howard, was a real diplomat, and always found a little "Indian blood" in anyone she sought to please. By the end of that weekend, Howard had come to believe that Winifred Black was divinely sent to him at precisely the right time to bring about the materialization of his dreams. On Black's last morning at the Lodge, when she came in to join Howard for breakfast, he involuntarily blurted out, "How beautiful you are this morning." Black was speechless. At a church service later that day, Black sat across the room from Howard, and quietly slipped out of the church house in the middle of the sermon to disappear without saying a word. Howard was broken-hearted. He practically worshiped Black and, in a later series of fawning letters between the two, he let it be known.

Howard had in mind a series of articles by Black that would focus on the Anglo-Saxon Mountaineer. He believed that he had exposed Black to a memorable weekend in his mountain retreat, but had little idea that it would be Granny Dollar that would capture Black's attention the most. Although Granny

Dollar had lived in Howard's spare cabin for almost five years, and he had amply supported her needs, including meat and tobacco, he had shown little-to-no interest in her story. Even after Sadie Shrader's article appeared in the regional agricultural magazine, *The Progressive Farmer* in January, he had only been inspired to mentioned Granny once[82] as a curiosity in his column.

In the middle of July, he received a letter from Winifred Black which included a sketch[83] that she had published in *The San Francisco Examiner* under the name Annie Laurie[84]. She had written an extensive feature on Granny Dollar, and it had been published in a paper with an international reach. Other papers began to pick up the story. Howard couldn't help but be interested. He was coming late to the party, but he was finally going to interview Granny for a proper article of his own[85].

In September, almost exactly five years after Granny Dollar arrived at the Master School, Howard, amidst a flurry of letter writing to Black, visited Granny at her cabin with a thought to "get an interesting story… little dreaming of the big vital message poor old Granny Dollar had for the world." But, it was also his intent to penetrate deeply into Granny's story, to try to ascertain something important. He had been mostly disinterested, skeptical even, but he was looking precisely for what he said he had little dream of discovering—a vital message. But, if Granny Dollar had a vital message to divulge, Howard didn't find it.

He discerned and acknowledged that Granny's primary claim-to-fame lay in her claim of great age. He estimated her to be around 106 in 1928[86], based on her descriptions of historical events that she "remembered." One of his goals was to verify her age to lend authenticity to her pioneer story. However, hearing what he wanted to hear in her responses, he easily deceived himself into believing that she was, notwithstanding her claims (and Sadie Shrader's published opinion), actually four years older. He also correctly determined that her place of birth was not Alabama but actually Georgia.[87]

Granny also provided additional details about her family. She claimed that her grandfather was John Grier Callahan and her great-grandfather was William Callahan.[88] Her great-grandmother Callahan married again, after the death of William, General Hugh Holland. Her father was a part of the band of "Chief McIntosh."[89] Granny had three half-brothers named Shadrach, Meshach, and Abednego, and three full-sisters named Roxie Ann, Georgie Ann, and Texie Ann.[90] The "Jukes" man, who caused her father's return to Georgia was sentenced to time in the penitentiary and his four sons were hanged. Other details included that well known DeKalb citizen, Griff Callahan[91] was a "distant cousin" of her father's; that she fought with a girl named Mary Pucket when she was a little girl, and Granny married Nelson Dollar[92] when she was 35 or 40 years old.

Beyond this information, Howard hit upon a few other details and facts about her family, childhood, religion, and livelihood—almost none of which can be readily checked against relevant records. There is no sign that Howard, despite his claim of skepticism, made any effort to authenticate her facts, or that he asked simple follow-up questions to flesh out her facts. Questions like who were her other siblings? Where did they live? When and where did they die? Who can verify her story? Did she have nieces and nephews? Given that she had no family support, this would have been a logical question for someone who was claiming to be the eldest of 26 siblings, many of whom were born a mere 30 miles away.

By focusing on Granny's two principal claims—her age, and her Indian heritage—Howard (as well as Shrader and Black) had missed her true story. Many of Granny's remembrances, as told by all three, are trite, stereotypical snapshots of supposed "Indian" life: the "Indian" removal at Fort Payne, struggles on the trail, women giving birth to children on the march, her family hiding out in a cave to avoid detection, etc. These types of stories have been told and retold where they have lost their context as to time and place. Therefore, they've become useless for either substantiating or refuting claims.

But Howard, if he suspected a deception, was in no mood to expose it. He relied upon these very "facts" to declare Granny's story authentic. Whenever she provided more detailed claims, those records that can either verify or falsify those claims, Howard dismissed them, stating, "Let the historian look this up and figure it out, and see what conclusion they arrive at." He went looking for "authenticity" and, as he wrote, "I got it." What he missed was the true, and truly fascinating, story of an authentic Appalachian granny woman.

"The folks keeps on comin' to be conjured"

Granny women were the ones others came to for healing and magic in the isolated mountains of Appalachia. Whenever illness or accidents struck, doctors weren't always available. But, there was always a granny woman nearby. Childbirth was a time of great concern and danger in the old days, and it was the granny woman who played an integral role in seeing that the baby and the mother survived.

These women combined their deep knowledge of old-world medical and magical techniques with knowledge of new world herbs and roots learned from their Cherokee and Creek neighbors. Their systems exhibited elements of European folk medicine, Greek classical medicine, Native American shamanism, West African traditional medicine, modern scientific medicine, sympathetic magic, and the faith-healing traditions of Christianity. They knew exactly the combinations of herbs and barks and which techniques to apply for each malady or injury.

Beyond health care, traditional granny magic included a lot

of different practices. For example, dowsing—the practice of looking for water with a forked stick or a length of copper—was a valuable skill to have if you or your neighbors needed to dig a new well. Granny women also practiced divination—reading tea leaves, watching for signs in the clouds, and other methods. They predicted weather, proposed proper times for planting and harvesting and interpreted omens or portents that guided day-to-day life such as marriage, travel, major investments, and other important events. But among all the skills of the granny woman, healing or otherwise, it was midwifery—assisting in the birth of babies, attending to the mother with remedies for pain (and the associated practice of birth control in the form of herbal remedies and other secret practices)—that was perhaps the most commonly used skill.

Practicing granny women guarded the secrets of their trade carefully, usually handing them down to only one person per generation. This was often treated as an apprenticeship that included secret ceremonies and mysterious rituals. Appalachian Granny folkways went by many names, depending on where it was practiced and who was doing the practicing: rootwork, folk medicine, folk magic, and kitchen witchery. Some would never think to call it anything but the work of faith and prayer. Milford Howard wrote that Granny Dollar "was a Christian who lived and practiced her Christianity." Granny referred to her faith-healing as "conjuring" and explained that conjuring was a practice of her Indian heritage, saying "conjuring is praying for us Indians….One who conjures cannot pray."[93] Whatever the name, granny magic is almost universally made up of herbal folk medicine, midwifery, omen-reading and fortune-telling, weather-working, and water-witching. The elixirs, potions, and practices of these women were the secrets of their trade. But their real power, in the minds of their clients, lay in their shaman-like, magico-religious powers of conjuring and their ability to convince the community that they could "see" and heal. Such powers came at great expense and they were not taken lightly.

To the Cherokee, old women played a special role in society. Cherokee males revered women and elevated them to positions of utmost respect and honor. Cherokee society also had great reverence and respect for the elderly. Thus, to the Cherokee, the elderly woman was the subject of great concern and, along with the children, entitled to the highest level of protection from the band.

When early Appalachian settlers came into contact with the Cherokee people, the exchange of health-care knowledge played an essential role in solidifying their relationships and molding their cultural practices. Europeans introduced the Cherokee to old world techniques, medicines, and rituals. In return, the Cherokee shared their knowledge of herbs and their methods of healing. The importance of the elderly woman became essential in establishing peaceful relations between the two societies.

For granny women, age is a badge of honor and a sign of wisdom. Even though it was not uncommon for southern women to become grandmothers in their thirties, those women practicing folk healing were affectionately called, "Granny." This reflected the expected age range of the practitioner and their immense store of wisdom and knowledge. So, it was not uncommon for them to exaggerate their age to add age and wisdom to their persona. John C. Campbell wrote, in *The Southern Highlander and His Homeland*, "There is something magnificent in many of the older women with their stern theology–part mysticism, part fatalism–and their deep understanding of life."

Most of the old granny women in those days could be spotted coming down the road smoking a cobbed pipe with a little black bag in their hand. Granny Dollar took on these images and evoked these sentiments in people. She was more of a mystic Christian than a textbook Christian, and she relied heavily on her pipe and her "Indian heritage" and "great age" to reinforce her "granny" persona.

Several references refer to Granny Dollar's practice of divination to support herself. It is important to understand that Granny Dollar's "fortune-telling" was an outgrowth of her religious practice—part of a religious ritual, invoking deities or spirits. Also, Granny Dollar's fortune-telling was likely restricted largely to predictions on matters such as weather and planting, as well as future romantic, financial, and childbearing prospects. Karen Cox, who researched and wrote *"Midwives and Granny Women"* for Foxfire 2 said that her research for that article was "startling" to her. Cox, like most modern readers, cannot easily imagine living in a community outside the range of clinics and hospitals.

In Albany, Georgia, a granny woman named Mary Coley, affectionately known as "Miss Mary," delivered over 3,000 babies during her 30-year career. Her story was presented in the 1952 documentary *"All My Babies: A Midwife's Own Story."*[94] Another well-known granny midwife was Rose Ellen Barbara Delilah Ingenthron of Taney County, Missouri (the granny woman tradition was equally common in the Ozark Mountain area). Ingenthron's mother was a midwife, who taught the trade to Rose. In the isolated area of Missouri that Ingenthron served, she was active as a midwife well into the 1980s. Her story is chronicled in her autobiography, *The Granny Woman of the Hills*[95].

Emma J. Smith, the wife of John Smith of Bankhead, on Lookout Mountain, was a noted midwife in the Mentone area in the 1890s through the early 1930s. Affectionately known as "Miss Emma J.", she served as postmistress until 1913 at a post office at her home farm Nightingale's post office. Known as the "mother of a community," she was part Cherokee, a mother of nine children, a feminist, a writer, a schoolteacher, and a midwife. [96]

Another local midwife, born in Walker County, Georgia in 1853, was Texas Frances Orleans Johnson. She married Jesse Johnson[97] in Dade County, Georgia in December 1873, and they lived on a farm at the upper end of Cove Road above the Blalock settlement on Lookout Mountain. "Aunt Tex," as she was known, had eleven children. She was a well-loved and well-respected midwife and herbalist doctor. She rode sidesaddle over the Mentone area in any kind of weather, day or night, to come to the aid of her neighbors in need.[98]

On Sand Mountain, near Macedonia, "Miss Biddie" Black Phillips was a noted midwife and folk healer. Her daughter

Opal once remarked that she felt bad for her eldest sister, Ora, since Ora had to raise all of her younger siblings. Their mother was away from home "all the time" delivering babies and sitting up with sick people.

In the late 19th and early 20th century, despite the significant importance and success of the informal midwife tradition, the state and federal governments, at the urging of progressive social reformers and medical professionals, instituted health care reforms to reduce infant mortality in isolated rural communities. Governments gathered statistics on infant mortality and enforced efforts to collect birth statistics and issue birth (and death) certificates. Government-funded clinics emerged, staffed with physicians and trained nurses.

The government promoted this activity in DeKalb County as early as the 1890s. Among their goals was to replace the role of granny midwife with trained nurses and doctors. However, there was much distrust of doctors in many of these rural communities. Finding they could not completely eradicate midwifery and home birth, reformers compromised by forcing traditional midwives to register with local health departments, attend classes at local midwife clubs, and obtain permits. Midwife clubs supported and regulated midwives. Public health nurses instructed pupils to maintain the clean-and-sterile standards required for practice. Midwife training focused on patient referral to clinics and reporting of births to the state agencies that issue birth certificates.

In *The Persecution and Prosecution of Granny Midwives in South Carolina, 1900–1940*, Sociologist Alicia D. Bonaparte documents how physicians actively advocated for the elimination of granny-midwives as childbirth grew increasingly medicalized. Consequently, as Bonaparte writes, "women of color suffered devaluation and stigmatization and came to be viewed as illegitimate medical practitioners." Under this regimen, practicing granny women, who were illiterate, were far less likely to survive the transition. This elimination of the granny woman was based on stereotypes, which were applied not only to the granny women but to all inhabitants of the Appalachian region.

Mary Willingham, an elderly African American granny nurse, and midwife received a certificate near Athens, Georgia in 1924 to assist doctors and midwives. She said, "It used to be, anybody could wait on a woman havin' a baby. They could go ahead and cut the cord if they knowed [sic] how. Now that's all changed. If you don't have a certificate, they'll put you in the penitentiary for life."[99]

In February 1895, the DeKalb County Board of Health reported that several midwives in the county had not been reporting the births and deaths that they had attended, "contrary to the law." The board threatened to bring these midwives to court to account for their actions. In 1909, the Alabama State Health Officer called for a meeting of all DeKalb County doctors and midwives at Fort Payne. The program called for the training of midwives in using "pen and ink" to document a child's name and birth statistics so that this documentation could accompany the report of the child's birth to the state. Further, the intent was to train midwives on hygiene and bacteriology.

Such topics would have seemed foreign and intimidating to the illiterate[100] Granny Dollar and there is no chance that she could have (or would have) attended such a meeting at Fort Payne. By 1920 the law required that only registered midwives could attend a birth, and officials encouraged parents to check with the board of health first, to ensure that they were engaging a registered midwife. These programs, as vital as they were for public health, had a devastating effect on granny midwives across Appalachia, particularly among women of color.

In 1910 there were more than 3,000 granny midwives in Georgia. By 1973, there were 196, with 85 of those being over the age of 65. The day of the granny midwife had peaked and was soon come to an end. Granny Dollar, an aging and illiterate granny woman found her midwife and medical skills less and less in demand. She started to rely more and more on fortune-telling to uphold her position in the community and earn a meager living. It's not surprising that, as time passed, the granny woman-midwife-folk healer persona became more and more legendary as memories of them faded[101].

"...eight miles east of Coffeetown"

Although Granny Dollar was subjected to multiple interviews, with her story having been covered in newspapers and magazines many times since her death, her chroniclers developed very little accurate information about her life. Most interviewers simply chose to believe the story they had come to hear. Most writers and commenters were careful to place hedge language into their articles and columns to address the unbelievable nature of her claims of extreme age. "Granny Dollar was what is known as a character," "assuming that all the information given by Granny Dollar in an interview in 1928 is factual...," and "Granny has quite an imagination, I can tell you" are all phrases used to express some level of skepticism in Granny's tales. According to Mentone historian Zora Shay Strayhorn, Granny "enjoyed embellishing the stories told about her and encouraged their telling."

Most articles and mentions published from 1928 until just before her death in January 1931 were rehashes of the original interviews with a bit of additional information, much of it inventions of the writer, introduced here and there. Since some information in various articles conflict, it is difficult, from the modern perspective, to understand which statements were original to Granny Dollar and which should be credited to the writers. For example, the claim that she was born in Buck's Pocket was not reported by Sadie Shrader or Winifred Black, and Howard wrote that Granny was born in Forsyth County, Georgia.

The information about Granny Dollar being born in Buck's Pocket seems to have first appeared in a newspaper article written by noted DeKalb historian Elizabeth S. Howard and James R. Kuykendall in 1982.[102] The article reported on an elderly DeKalb County resident who told a story of Indians returning to Buck's Pocket after their forced removal from Alabama in the 1830s. The story stated outright that Granny Dollar was "born in Buck's Pocket in the early 1820s." Until this time, Granny Dollar's birthplace had been consistently reported as "eight miles east of Coffeetown." By the 1920s, Buck's Pocket was known to have been occupied by the Cherokee in earlier times, and there are many signs that it served as one of their principal encampments and hunting grounds. By that time it was being heavily farmed and, due to its remoteness and road conditions in the county, numerous illegal whiskey stills were operating there. But, its reputation as a Cherokee refuge was already well known. There was evidence of their presence found, carvings of snakes and fowl, on rocks, and birches that lined Sauty Creek.

Across the river from the mouth of Buck's Pocket lay Sauta Cave. As early as 1784, the soil of the cave floor was being mined by the Cherokee to make saltpeter, an ingredient in black powder. The mining continued on and off from the War of 1812 through the Civil War. Granny Dollar's claim that her family had hidden out in a saltpeter cave to avoid forced removal may have led to the natural association of this cave and nearby Buck's Pocket. The cave was highly trafficked as it had served as the Jackson County Courthouse in 1819-1820 and was being operated as a nightclub in the 1920s[103]. But, it is unlikely that a family of Indians could hide in such a spot, even in the late 1830s. Records also confirm that her family did not hide out there to evade forced removal to the west.

Granny Dollar would have known of the reputation of Buck's Pocket as a home of Indians, whether or not she was born there. She could have reported that, but it is more likely that this information was introduced much later in the telling and retelling of her legend. It is also likely that writers such as Howard and Kuykendall unintentionally linked information from many undocumented sources to Granny Dollar. Records show that she was not born in Buck's Pocket.

It is also likely, if not clear, that some information provided by Granny Dollar was elicited from her to challenge her story or dig deeper into it. For example, after telling Shrader how her father had refused to leave his homeland in Alabama to go west with his clan, she nonchalantly advised that he "later left for Georgia." Shrader challenged the logic of this statement and was rewarded with a detailed story of how he fled to Georgia after a vicious, but well-justified fight with a murderous white man, named Jukes. Also, when Howard later suggested the possibility that Juke's real name was Dukes, a more likely name with bonafide DeKalb County links, Granny held firm to her story. Records do not support a Jukes family living in DeKalb

County or Jackson County during the time of interest.

In reality, much of the information provided by Granny Dollar, or subsequently introduced about her, establishes very little surrounding her actual life. From the various interviews, and subsequent stories and myths, the following potentially historical claims are clear:

1. She was born in Alabama around 1822 in Buck's Pocket(E. Howard) or "about 8 miles east of Coffeetown" (Shrader).[104] Alternatively, she was born in July 1827 in Forsyth County, Georgia (M. Howard).
2. Her name was Nancy Callahan, the eldest child of William Callahan (a "full-blooded" Cherokee), and Mary Sexton (of Cherokee and Irish descent) (Shrader). Alternatively, Mary Sexton was a Scott (M. Howard).
3. Granny's father was a part of the Band of Chief McIntosh (M. Howard)
4. Her grandfather was John Grier Callahan (M. Howard).
5. Her great-grandfather was William Callahan (M. Howard).
6. Her great-grandmother married Gen. Hugh Holland (M. Howard).
7. Her father had two wives at the same time, Mary Sexton and Cassie, each with their own families (Shrader, M. Howard).
8. Altogether her father sired 26 children by his two wives, plus many other illegitimate children (Shrader, M. Howard).
9. She had a neighbor named Victor who had two wives named Hettie and Charlotte (Shrader).

10. Her father served the U. S. in the "Indian War[105]" (M. Howard).
11. Her father got into a dispute in Alabama around 1840 with a man named Jukes (Shrader, M. Howard), who served time in the penitentiary (M. Howard). His four sons were all hanged (M. Howard).
12. Her family moved to a small town about 30 miles from Marthasville (Atlanta), Georgia around 1840 (Shrader).
13. Her mother gave birth to three sets of triplets.[106] (Shrader, M. Howard)
14. One of his father's two wives died before she (Nancy) turned 21 years old (around 1845) (Shrader). Her father's wife, Cassie, died after giving birth to triplets (M. Howard).
15. At around 21 years of age, Nancy hauled goods for a company known as Kyle Brothers Wholesalers.[107]
16. She delivered goods to a merchant named George Pass (Shrader).
17. She was engaged to a man named Tom Porter who was the son of a merchant near Atlanta, and who died during the Civil War.
18. Her father served in the Civil War and died at the battle of Atlanta.
19. Madge Cole and her five children lived with Nancy for three years (M. Howard).
20. She returned to Alabama and married Nelson Dollar "about 40 years after the Civil War ended" when she was 79 years old (Shrader). She married Nelson Dollar when she was around 35 or 40 years old (M. Howard).
21. All of her siblings died prior to January 1928[108] (Shrader).
22. She had three half-brothers named Shadrach, Meshach,

and Abednego (M. Howard).
23. She had three sisters named Roxie Ann, Georgie Ann, and Texie Ann (M. Howard).
24. She was distantly related to Griff Callahan, the son of a prominent citizen of DeKalb County, Alabama (M. Howard).

It would be naïve to believe that no reporter or researcher has ever undertaken the effort of looking into the story of Granny Dollar. It is equally unlikely that no one in DeKalb County, at the time that Granny Dollar lived, wondered and asked about her family, particularly when she was gravely ill. In fact, *The Fort Payne Journal*, on March 27, 1929, included a snippet on page 6 that read, "Granny Dollar is very ill at this writing. Her recovery is doubtful. Mr. and Mrs. T. N. Gray[109] were among the visitors at Granny Dollar's Sunday." Milford Howard, in his column, reported that two prominent DeKalb County citizens were related to her and reported the name of one, Griff Callahan. The fact that such publications, almost two years prior to her actual death, did not elicit concerned inquiries by relatives would have been puzzling to a community that faithfully believed her story. Even if her 25 siblings were dead, would they not have left nieces and nephews? But, as Milford Howard pointed out, it was two of her claims that first caught the attention of the readers: her Indian heritage, and extreme age.

"You know, I'm an "injun"

When she emerged from obscurity in 1923, Granny Dollar did not make any extraordinary claims. She had no intention of seeking publicity, much less establishing herself as a legend and myth. She had no story to sell. She only sought the support of her neighbors. Having become a widow only four or five months earlier, she found herself with few options. So, she arrived at the Master School seeking help. In part to endear herself to the boys and girls of the schools, and also to ensure her welcome there, Granny repeated a common claim—that she was "Indian." Since that time, Granny Dollar's story has appeared in numerous publications as an example of how Native Americans lived, and were treated, in Alabama after the forced removal[110]. But how true was her story?

Claims of Native American heritage, as any Southerner is aware, are not uncommon. Every semester, students enrolled in Native American studies at universities across the South boast of having Cherokee heritage[111]. Every year, hundreds of high school students write theme papers based on their own presumed Cherokee heritage. The tradition of claiming a Cherokee ancestor is more than a hundred years old and continues in the present. Today, more Americans claim descent from Cherokee ancestry, than any other Native American group. Tales of family genealogies become murkier with each passing generation, but contemporary Americans continue to profess their belief despite having no evidence to prove Cherokee ancestry. This phenomenon can be traced back to the 19th century.

By 2010, the U. S. Census Bureau reported that more than 800,000 Americans claimed at least one Cherokee ancestor. DNA research has shown that European-American genomes, as of 2020, contain just 0.18% Native American DNA. However, many of these claims may have had a hint of truth to them. In the late 17th and early 18th centuries, it was common for Cherokees to intermarry outside their clan. For diplomatic reasons, Cherokees of this period often took European spouses. Additionally, many European traders sought to solidify their relationships with the Cherokees through marriage into the clan. Although the Cherokee were historically generous in enrolling people into their tribal membership, the Eastern Band of Cherokee Indians today restricts enrollment to people with a direct lineal ancestor who appears on the 1924 Baker Roll[112] of the Eastern Band of Cherokee Indians. This ancestor also has to possess at least 1/16 degree of Eastern Cherokee blood[113].

Historically, the Cherokee people settled across the entire breadth of the southern Appalachian mountains from Ohio to the north, the Savannah River's headwaters to the southeast, and possibly as far west as Muscle Shoals, Alabama. Cherokee representatives in 1817, including the Georgia bands, relinquished their territories to the United States. In exchange, the 1817 treaty called for those wishing to stay to receive their home and 640 acres of land. However, the United States government failed to enforce this provision. This decision ultimately led to the forced removal of the Cherokee people (except for the Oconaluftee and Euchella bands in North Carolina) from their homelands. The continued existence of the eastern band of the Cherokee, who were considered to be US citizens, along with the numerous Cherokee 'fugitives' who had evaded the forced removal, created a confusing legal state regarding citizenship. In 1897, the US Supreme Court ruled that the Cherokees in the east, including those previously considered to be citizens as well as those deemed fugitives, were a single tribe, the Eastern Band of the Cherokee.[114]

The population of Cherokees in Georgia and Alabama was never substantial. By 1835, most of the Cherokee in Georgia were concentrated in Gilmer, Lumpkin, Floyd, and Union counties. Additional populations were scattered from Blue Ridge and Tocoa to the Etowah River near Rome. Smaller populations also ranged into western Alabama. Until 1970, the population of Georgia Cherokees enumerated by the US Census remained in the few hundreds. Beginning with the 1970 Census, however, the numbers skyrocketed. This wasn't a reflection of growth in the originally enumerated population, but rather it was a result of a new policy. In 1970, the US Census Bureau started the practice of counting "self-designated" Indians.

Genealogists have encountered the various censuses of Cherokee and Creek peoples, many of which were primarily associated with the federal government's reparations payment. These government payment programs, as one can imagine, evoked many false claims. For example, the Guion-Miller roll of the early 20th century documented over 125,000 Cherokee ancestry claims, with only around 30,000 (less than 25%) of those claimants eventually approved to receive payments. Of course, not all the rejected claims were fraudulent. The Cherokee rejected claims for many reasons.

When Granny Dollar's brother-in-law, William Michael Waters, applied for inclusion in the Eastern Band of Cherokees in 1926, he wrote that his mother was a full Cherokee named Mary Luns[115]. William also cited five Cherokee first cousins who still lived among the Eastern Band Cherokees in North Carolina. Such stories indicate the complexity of Cherokee affiliation.

The tribe ultimately rejected William Waters' application for reasons unassociated with his mother's "degree of blood." Among the reasons given for the claim's dismissal was that his ancestor had, for many years, lived apart from the Cherokees and had not contributed monetarily to the band's purchase of their Qualla tribal land. Essentially, the board considered any right of Cherokee citizenship that Waters may have held to have been forfeited or lost due to non-affiliation, a circumstance that has nothing to do with blood/DNA and everything to do with culture.

Indian identity has always been a developing subject. Many factors have been used to define "Indianness," culture, society, genes/biology, law, and self-identity. Also, the definition has been dynamic across time. With Granny Dollar, it is not clear how much her identity relied on her DNA, and how much relied on her culture and self-identity. The Cherokee were traditionally generous in granting tribal membership to others, particularly those married into the tribe. Sometimes, the opposite situation occurred with a white couple adopting Cherokee orphans and raising their children primarily among white society.

There is no way of knowing the number of Cherokees who married Europeans during the early 1800s in Georgia. Traditionally, language has also been seen as an essential part of identity, and learning the Cherokee language was considered an important part of tribal life. When the great-grandchildren of Abel Peek and his Cherokee wife, Peggy, applied for membership into the Cherokee tribe in DeKalb County in the early 1900s, they cited their grandfather's ability to speak the Cherokee language as one factor to authenticate their ancestry. Another factor affecting tribal affiliation was participation in sacred traditions shared by the Cherokee people.

The Cherokee never had permanent territory within the boundaries of Gwinnett County. Cherokees only arrived west of the Chattahoochee River following the Treaty of 1793. After that, the Cherokee population was relatively sparse near Gwinnett County[116]. But, Cherokees were living in nearby Forsyth Count, in reasonably large numbers. With Granny Dollar, it is impossible to determine any accurate quantitative value for the degree of blood inherited from Cherokee ancestors, but she was certainly exposed to the Cherokee culture. Research shows that her parents and known grandparents had western names and lived in western society for many years within three miles of the Cherokee homelands border and inside the boundaries of the Creek homelands. There are traditions within the families of at least some of her siblings (or half-siblings) that support Cherokee heritage. However, neither she nor any of her known ancestors appear on the Baker roll[117]. Her half-sister Milly appears in an affidavit signed by her husband (William Michael Waters) in May 1926, having 1/4 (degree of blood) Cherokee ancestry[118]. However, it is not clear what portion of that ancestry was contributed by Milly's (and Nancy's) father or by Milly's mother, Catherine Brown.

Besides self-identifying as a Cherokee, Granny Dollar is known[119] to have taken part in some (claimed) Cherokee rituals and sacred traditions, including traditional Cherokee medicine, sacred songs, and funerary rites. Given her half-sister's claims, it is reasonable to conclude that Nancy Dollar was likely, at most, 1/4 Cherokee and that her Cherokee lineage, if she had any at all, was through her paternal grandmother. It is unlikely that Nancy could have qualified for formal inclusion to the Baker Roll and the Eastern Band of the Cherokees.

"...out of my baby ways"

Similar to claims of Native American ancestry, unsubstantiated claims of extreme longevity are not uncommon. The Guinness World Records has stated that "No single subject is more obscured by vanity, deceit, falsehood, and deliberate fraud than the extremes of human longevity." Before the 19th century, there was insufficient evidence either to demonstrate or to refute centenarian longevity. In the early 20th century, while records existed, there were insufficient processes for getting access to the evidence to verify (or to refute) such claims. Consequently, in the early 20th century, such exaggerated claims of longevity were very common.

In 1907, Sarah Gibson passed away in Celera, Alabama at age 89. Her death was noteworthy, not because of her age, but because she was the wife of the oldest reported citizen in Alabama, Austin Gibson. Austin was reported to be 119 years old when his wife passed away. But just seven years earlier, Austin Gibson had reported his age as 101 on the 1900 US Census. Even if that date were accurate, it would mean that he was no more than 108 at the time of his wife's passing. Analysis of the 1840 and 1870 censuses indicates that Austin Gibson was not born before 1810. He was most likely born in July 1814. This would make his age 93 at the time his wife passed. Why would the Gibsons lie about their age? The Gibsons had been exhibited in fairs around the state for years, billed as the oldest couple in the state. Such claims are common. So too are the patterns of birth dates being gradually exaggerated as the person making the claim ages. In the Gibsons' case, their income was, in part, dependent on an exaggerated age.

In March of 1903, Marsylla Keith of Mobile, Alabama celebrated her 116th birthday. According to reports, Keith claimed to have vivid memories of times before the War of 1812. However, records do not support anyone named Marsylla Keith living in Mobile, Alabama. Interestingly, Marsylla was also reported to be living in Montgomery, West Virginia by many newspapers across the country. This case highlights another issue with reports of extreme age. In some cases, newspapers have an interest in exaggerating the ages of the citizens they report on. Whether the city that Keith was living in was intentionally hidden, or the result of the vagueness in such reports, is unknown. Keith appears in an earlier paper, however.

On December 17, 1900, an article appeared in *The Nashville American* newspaper about "Old Granny Keith," as she was called, being 111 years old and "possibly the oldest person in the world." At that time, she was living with her daughter at 406 Herron Street in Montgomery, Alabama. According to that paper, she came to Montgomery at 15 with her father, Mr. Lewis, from South Carolina. There she met and married Mr. Keith. They made their home on Pintlala Creek and had thirteen children. Mr. Keith died at the age of 62. An article in *The Montgomery Advertiser* on April 30, 1903, announced her death and listed her husband as James Washington Keith, her father as Edmund Lewis, and her mother as Nancy Williams. According to the article, Marsylla Lewis was born in Darlington, South Carolina, and migrated to Alabama with her parents when she was about 15. She married James Keith when she was 25 years old, "just before the war of 1812". That article claimed that James and his two brothers left to fight for the US in that war. James died in 1862 at the age of 85.

With all the newspaper coverage regarding Marsylla Keith, it might be thought that some reliable research had been done by some writer or editor. Pension records indicate that Marsylla Keith filed a pension application as a widow seeking a pension for her husband's War of 1812 service. However, authorities could find no such soldier named James Keith. Furthermore, the 1860 US Census indicates that Marsylla Keith was born in 1810, making her 93 years old at her death rather than 111. In the 1880 census, Marsylla was listed as 72 years old, making her no more than 95 at her death. It is uncertain why Marsylla Keith would claim to be more than 25 years older than she was. But, it likely involved her and her husband's effort to qualify for a War of 1812 pension that he may not have earned.

A man named Charlie Smith emerged in 1955, claiming to be 108 years old and born in 1847. At the time, he was residing in Florida and working as a fruit picker. After being informed by Social Security officials that they had an affidavit in their files stating that he was born in 1842, he adopted that earlier date as his birth year; this instantly made him 113 years old. Smith, like Granny Dollar, was known for telling tall tales. He became a variety store owner, getting significant media attention as he was touted as the oldest man in the US. He toured with circuses and was prominently featured in *Ripley's Believe It or Not!*. Unfortunately for Smith, he would live until 1979 and each year that passed would bring more and more doubt to his claims. In 1978, an investigation thoroughly debunked his claimed age. Both his 1910 marriage certificate and the 1910 census listed him as age 35, making him, at most, 105 at the time of his death and barely over 80 when he first emerged claiming to be 113. In Charlie Smith's case, it appears that the exaggeration of his age was driven less by economic factors and more by his personality as a teller of tall tales.

In Panama City, Florida, in August 1951, Leonard "Bud" Finch prepared for his first airplane flight, reportedly at age 111. He wanted to see what the cabin where he had lived for "more than 100 years" looked like from "up yonder." Unfortunately, Finch's son vetoed the flight, thinking the stress would be too much for his father. Bud expressed the hope to take the flight on his 112th birthday in a year. The 1940 U. S. Census listed Leonard Finch as 98 years old, making him 109 years old at the time of his canceled flight. Finch died on January 4, 1955, and was reported to be 111 still. But, in 1900, Finch was listed as making him 103 at his death. He also appears in the 1860 Census at age 8, making him 99 years old at the time of his attempted flight and still an impressive 102 years old at the time of his death. But, he was nowhere near the 115 years claimed for him when he passed away.

In DeKalb County, on Sand Mountain, in 1879, an elderly

black woman showed up at the courthouse to plead with the court to remove her name from the pauper's list. She was Ann Bynum, a formerly enslaved woman called "Old Aunt Ann." Her family had placed her on the pauper's list a few years earlier because they could no longer care for her. In a story somewhat reminiscent of Granny Dollar's tale, she had walked six miles to appear at the court to insist that she could care for herself because she feared the label of "pauper." A year earlier, a Gadsden, Alabama newspaper reported her age at 128 years old. A year after she showed up in court and two years after the Gadsden article, she was recorded in the 1880 US Census. She was living as a boarder in George Foster's home, and Census taker A. G. Bennett was stunned to hear that she was 121 years old. In efforts to double-check her story, he found witnesses there who would claim that they had seen a bill-of-sale for her when she was still a slave, which would indicate that her age was at 128.

Notwithstanding those witnesses' statements, ten years earlier, in 1870, she told another DeKalb County Census taker she was 100 years old, meaning that she had aged either 21 years or 28 years (depending on sources) in one decade. Ten years earlier still, in the 1860 Census, she reported her age as 73. In 1850, the oldest female slave owned by her previous owner William Bynum (likely Ann) in DeKalb County, Alabama, was only 55 years old. So, it is likely that she was born in Virginia (as stated in the census) between 1787 and 1795. In 1880, when she reported her age as 121 and the Gadsden Newspapers calculated her age at 130, she was actually no more than 93 years old and possibly as young as 85.

There are many reasons for people to exaggerate their age. In rural communities like DeKalb County, Alabama, in the late 1800s and early 1900s, a phenomenon known as age-heaping is one likely contributor. Before the twentieth century, age mattered little, and people were asked their ages on relatively rare occasions. Documentation of age was also more irregular, as birth certificates, drivers' licenses, and passports did not exist. Age-heaping occurs when largely illiterate people are required to provide their age. The tendency, in these circumstances, is for the person to simply round their age up or down to the nearest 5 or 10 years since it would be difficult for them to calculate their age from a specific birth year. If age-heaping continued over many years and multiple occurrences, it was possible for someone to forget their birth year altogether, or accidentally add a decade to their already estimated age. Of course, there were also many situations in which someone might benefit from being older. For example, to avoid military service, qualify for a pension, justify retirement, or avoid embarrassing circumstances, such as marriage at an unusually early age or an age-mismatch in their marriage. Also, extreme age brings attention, and newspapers may even contribute to the exaggeration. There is little actual harm in an elderly person getting a little attention for their age. With Granny Dollar, the claim of great age likely brought a reputation of wisdom, which served, along with her claim of Indian heritage, to enhance her reputation as a midwife, healer, and fortune-teller[120][121].

We know that Granny Dollar did not exaggerate her age to cover for marrying at an unusually early age because she did not marry until late in life. When she married, she married a fellow Lookout Mountain resident from her hometown, Nelson Dollar, Jr.

"I got me a good man"

In 1899, Alabama passed a law providing public pensions to former Confederate soldiers and their widows. Before that time, pension payments were limited to disabled veterans, specifically those with lost limbs or sight. In February of that year, they expanded the law to include veterans who were indigent and unable to work due to age. It was probably between 1893 and 1899 that Nelson Dollar, Jr., a lifelong Georgia resident, and a Confederate veteran, moved from Forsyth County, Georgia, to DeKalb County. A key motivation for the move was to take advantage of this series of increasingly liberal pension laws. Georgia's pension laws were more strict, and Dollar had other reasons to avoid Georgia's review board process—he was a deserter from a Georgia artillery battalion. Nancy, who had lived with Nelson Dollar since 1893, joined him in making this move to DeKalb County, Alabama, but the date of this move is uncertain. In 1906, Nelson Dollar, Jr., filed a petition for a pension and swore that he was a resident of Alabama on January 1, 1899. However, he provided false information on the pension application regarding his service, so it isn't necessary to assume that he lived in Alabama. Both he and Nancy appear on the 1900 US Census, living on Lookout Mountain in DeKalb County. Also migrating to Lookout

Mountain, in DeKalb County, along with Nelson Dollar and Nancy, was Nancy's sister, California Savannah Johnson, her husband, William Thomas Johnson, and their seven children. The Johnsons settled nearby (about three miles north of the Dollars) at Fischer's Mill, which would later become River Park.

Granny Dollar told various stories about the date of her only marriage.[122] To Sadie Shrader, she said that she married about 40 years after the Civil War (i. e., 1905), at 79. She told Milford Howard that she married when she was about "35 or 40 years old" (no date specified). She told census-takers in 1900 that she married in 1894 at age 54, and again in 1910 that she married in 1893 at age 56. She didn't specify her age to Winifred Black when recounting her marriage to Nelson Dollar, but she claimed to have had children of her own with him, showing that she was young enough to have done so. In reality, records show that she married Nelson Dollar on October 5, 1909, in Walker County, Georgia, when she was 61 years old and he was 74.

Walker County, Georgia is the northernmost Georgia County on Lookout Mountain. Nelson and Nancy Dollar lived near Kensington, about 25 miles north of Mentone, Alabama, for several years. The discrepancy in her reported dates is likely due to her reluctance to disclose that she and Nelson Dollar had lived together as man and wife for at least 16 years before being married.[123] They were likely living together as man and wife as early as 1893,[124] shortly Nelson Dollar's first wife's death when Nancy was 43 years old (an age not inconsistent with what she told Milford Howard). When they did eventually marry, it was to ensure that Nancy would receive Nelson Dollar's Confederate pension if he were to die.

Nelson Dollar was born in Gwinnett County, Georgia, November 2, 1835.[125] He was the great-grandson of the Revolutionary War patriot Reuben Dollar and Mary Ann Wilbanks. Reuben Dollar had migrated from Wales, first to South Carolina and then to Georgia, after 1784. He and his wife were the progenitors of many related Dollar families in the Gwinnett and Forsyth County area of Georgia in the early to mid-1800s. Nelson had brothers named Ruben, James, John, Noah, Pinkney[126], and Lafayette. His father was Nelson "Nelse" Sr.

In the 1850s, there was a renewed interest in mining gold in nearby Dahlonega, Georgia. Nelson left his home in Gwinnett County, when he was between 15 and 19 years old and went to the north Georgia area to work as a gold miner. When he returned to Gwinnett County before April 1861, many of the men of that county and neighboring Forsyth county were enlisting, in a fever of southern patriotism, in the provisional army of the Confederate States. Nelson Dollar, who would have been between 27 and 30 years old, was of age and would have been expected to serve in the regular army. As the war began, Georgia held volunteers who were under 18 and over 35 back as a reserve force and enrolled them in the state militia units rather than the regular army. Nelson first attempted to enlist for six months in Company F of the 6th Georgia State troops, the home guard unit of his father. But they soon transferred him to the 12th Battalion, Light Artillery of the Regular Confederate Army, which was mustered in Savannah,

Georgia.

In December 1861, with the end of the war nowhere in sight, the Confederate authorities were facing the loss of 148 regiments, or nearly half the army, when their 1-year enlistments expired in March 1862. The Confederate Congress attempted to induce reenlistment by offering bounties, a sixty-day furlough, and the option of joining a new regiment with new elections of officers. Although General Robert E. Lee would later pronounce this a disastrous policy, and argue compulsory conscription was essential to win the war, it was implemented for a short time. Nelson Dollar would take advantage of that briefly active policy and reenlist for a three-year term.

On April 23, 1862, while mustered in Savannah with his 12th (Light Artillery) Battalion, he transferred to the newly organized Company D of the 9th Battalion of Georgia Artillery (The Gwinnett Artillery). He mustered back near his home in Lawrenceville, Georgia. Nelson Dollar was one of 149 privates initially stationed with Company D at Camp Luckey to await arming and provisioning and to act as guards for government stores at Atlanta. On July 1, 1863, the now-provisioned Company marched to Knoxville, Tennessee. They briefly saw service in Virginia, including Saltville, before returning to Knoxville. Then, on August 23, they set out on foot for Lafayette, Georgia. On September 17, again on foot, the Company marched to Chickamauga, Georgia, and was attached to Preston's Division of Buckner's Corps. On September 19 and September 20, 1863, they took part in the Battle of Chickamauga protecting a ridge near Chickamauga

Creek with two twelve-pound Napoleon cannons, two twenty-four-pound howitzers, and sixty-nine pounds of ammunition.

On September 27, seven days after the end of the bloody battle of Chickamauga, the Confederate Congress would act again. In addition to extending the age limit to 45, they would change the service period from three years to "an unlimited period." Suddenly, for men like Nelson Dollar, some of whom had enlisted for only one year (and had almost served that year), their enlistment periods, first extended to three years, was now "the length of the war", however long that might be. Meanwhile, men of means could still get out of serving by paying an able-bodied man who was otherwise not subject to conscription to take their place. Also, anyone wealthy enough to own 20 or more slaves was exempted completely. Of course, Confederate and state officials were careful to exempt themselves as well. Also exempted were Christian ministers, teachers, druggists, doctors, and many other skilled professionals, while farmers bore the brunt of fighting the war. Eventually, the 9th Georgia Artillery would fight in Georgia, Tennessee, Kentucky, and Virginia, finally surrendering at Appomattox. But, Nelson Dollar would not be there. By this time, the Confederate conscription act, which was always controversial in Georgia, was so unpopular that it was almost impossible to enforce. According to military records, on the night of October 31, 1863, under a nearly full moon, Nelson Dollar quietly slipped out of camp and returned to his home in Gwinnett County[127].

On June 28, 1865, two months after the end of hostilities, Nelson Dollar emerged from his low profile life to marry Emily Burton, the 18-year-old daughter of Elias Burton and Mary

Ann Dodd in Cumming, Forsyth County, Georgia. Nelson would claim his age as 21, but he was more than 30 at the time. Nelson and Emily would go on to have five children, three sons, and two daughters. All of the Dollar children settled and remained in Forsyth and Hall Counties of Georgia. Nelson's wife, Emily died in Sugar Hill, Georgia in 1891. Sometime after that, probably around 1893, Nelson and Nancy began to cohabitate. Then, together, they left their lifelong homes and headed for Alabama[128].

In February 1906, Nelson Dollar applied to the Alabama State Board of Examiners to be placed on Alabama's pension rolls. A DeKalb County board, made up of physician William E. Quin and veteran J. R. Jones, approved his application and forwarded it to the state board of examiners in Montgomery. On August 15, 1906, Nelson Dollar was placed on the pension rolls as a 4th class pensioner earning $12.50 per month. By April 1913, seven years later, Dollar had been moved to a third-class pensioner, and that amount had increased to $16.00 per month. On August 21, 1913, Nelson Dollar appeared at the DeKalb County Probate Court and appealed to the State pension board to be reclassified (on account of age) as a class 2 pensioner, a move that would earn him $4.00 more per month. The decision to request this increase would prove disastrous for both Nelson and Granny Dollar.

Claims for Confederate pensions in Alabama were assessed by a county board of examiners, appointed by the governor, consisting of one "practicing physician of good standing in his profession" and one Confederate veteran "of good moral character." This system's purpose was to ensure that men (and widows) earning pensions were worthy, and state legislators believed that this type of moral evaluation could best be carried out at a local level. However, despite these efforts, there is evidence of corruption among county pension boards from the historical record. One Alabama state audit board complained about local adjudication practices, writing, "This effort of the State to aid these worthy men is being sadly abused. Applications are allowed in a great many instances that should be rejected." Auditors complained that local boards[129], in some counties, did not fully appreciate the trust placed in them and were accused of granting applications that they knew were based on false statements.

On April 1, 1864, the Alabama State Board of Pensioners did what the local DeKalb County board had failed to do. They sent a letter to Nelson Dollar accusing him of desertion and giving him 20 days to appear before Montgomery's board to defend himself. Dollar responded to the board by saying that he was old and unable to defend himself against the charges. He asked the board to refer to his previously provided "proof" of his service, which had amounted to two affidavits sworn by men of Forsyth County, Georgia. Both falsely claimed that they knew Nelson Dollar to have served for the entire length of the war. On July 2, 1914, *the Fort Payne Journal* reported that Nelson Dollar, along with 63 other DeKalb County men, was dropped from the confederate pension rolls. The move would have been of small consequence for Nelson Dollar, since, as Milford Howard reported, he usually spent his entire pension on whiskey. According to Howard, Nelson Dollar was "a sorry sort," but Granny idealized him. Howard believed that Granny could have pursued the issue, but "knowing something of political red tape," he didn't have the energy to pursue it on her behalf. For Granny Dollar, the loss would be overwhelming. For nine years, she would "fight life's battles" without that pension and would end up as an aged widow, alone with no means of support. When he died in 1923, Nelson Dollar was 88 years old.

II

Part II

"There is a history in all men's lives." William Shakespeare, Henry IV Part II

"My father's hut was enjoyed by all"

So, what facts can we confirm about Granny Dollar? Granny was born Nancy Emeline Callaway[130] (not Callahan[131]) in June 1848 in Sugar Hill, Gwinnett County, Georgia to William Anderson Callaway and Mary Garrett (Sexton) Callaway. She was the fourth child (the third to survive infancy) of the couple, who were married in Gwinnett County on March 24, 1844. Nancy lived for the majority of her life, from her birth until around 1893, in the area of Sugar Hill, Georgia with her parents her siblings, and her grandparents. When she died in January 1931, Granny Dollar was 82 1/2 years old.

Sugar Hill is the northernmost town in Gwinnett County. The Callaway family were early residents of the area. In 1818, the state of Georgia, to honor the three Georgia men who signed the Declaration of Independence, established three counties: Hall County, named for Lyman Hall; Walton County, named for George Walton; and Gwinnett County, named for Button Gwinnett. The counties were formed from parts of Jackson County (formerly part of Franklin County) and lands gained through the cession of Creek Indian lands. One of the earliest white settlements was on the Apalachee River (near its source) at Hog Mountain near Sugar Hill.

In 1820, the state of Georgia undertook the third Georgia Land Lottery to distribute lands to these newly formed counties. Land lotteries were an early nineteenth-century system of land redistribution used in Georgia and other states. Under the land lottery system, white male citizens could register for a chance to win lots, or parcels of land that had been forcibly taken from the Creek and Cherokee peoples. The 1820 land lottery included the redistribution of a large section of land in northwest Georgia, including Gwinnett County. Among the fortunate drawers in this lottery were the "orphans of William Callaway," John, Martin, and James Callaway[132]. For the registration fee of around $18, the Callaway orphans received 250 acres on Shoal Creek, in northern Gwinnett County, in the area known as Sugar Hill. Their father, William Callaway, had been born around 1783 in Wilkes County, Georgia[133]. He was part of a large Callaway clan who lived at Rayle, Georgia, about 9 miles west of the town of Washington. William's will had been probated in Wilkes County in 1819[134]. He died sometime between 1816 and 1819. Meanwhile, his orphans moved about 50 miles southwest of Rayle to Indian Creek, in Putnam County, Georgia. It is possible that they were living with their mother, who may have remarried, or with a wealthy cousin of their father's,[135] John Callaway, Jr.[136]

Of the orphans, John Callaway was born around 1803 in Jasper County, Georgia. His brother Martin Kinny Callaway was born about 2 years later, and the youngest, James Callaway was born in 1808. John Callaway married Mary Elizabeth "Betsy" McCarter in Jasper County, Georgia on March 23, 1823. John and Betsy had only one child who survived childhood[137], a son, William Anderson Callaway[138]. He was born in Jasper County on May 26, 1825.[139] John's brother, Martin Kinny Callaway married Eliza Louise Smith in Jasper County, on December 28, 1826. He went west and settled in Arkansas. But, John Callaway, sometime between 1826 and 1833, settled in Sugar Hill on the land that the brothers won in the lottery. The youngest brother, James Callaway, after moving to Meriwether County and marrying, also migrated to Sugar Hill.

Sugar Hill is today, a suburb of Atlanta. It is bordered to the northeast by the city of Buford and to the southwest by the city of Suwanee. In the 1840s a road led from Lawrenceville, the Gwinnett county seat, to Cumming, the county seat of neighboring Forsyth County. Sugar Hill lay on that road almost precisely 11 miles from each county seat. Sugar Hill also lay in the middle of a road from the rail town of Buford, northeast of Sugar Hill, to Cumming. According to the story, a freight wagon traveling from the railroad in Buford to Cumming broke a wheel while traversing a steep hill spilling its load of sugar all over the hill, and that is where the town got its name. Sugar Hill also lay on a popular ford of the Chattahoochee River. Sugar Hill was a lively place in the 1840s and was intimately connected to the towns that lay at either end of its main roads.

In 1833, Island Ford Baptist Church,[140] a rough-hewn log building, was constructed in the woods near the Chattahoochee River, in northwest Gwinnett County near a place where people forded the river. The crossing traversed an island half a mile wide, and this gave the church its name. It was organized in February, with John Callaway among the founding members, and was the first church in Gwinnett County. John Callaway had recently settled on Lot 349 in District 7. The lot, which spanned Shoal Creek a mile or so from the Chattahoochee River, was the one that he and his brothers won in the land lottery. According to Callaway family tradition, John had a very large estate in Gwinnett and was the owner of more than 90 slaves before the Civil War, all of which he lost in the reconstruction[141]. By 1850 John Callaway owned two farms. One, of 187 acres (80 acres were in cultivation), was valued at more than $2,000. The second, of 55 acres (20 acres were in cultivation), was valued at less than $300 and was likely the farm where William and his family lived. The Callaways, at least by this time, did not own slaves[142]. By the time John Callaway died in 1891, and his wife died in 1898, the estate was 392 acres[143].

Granny Dollar idealized her father, just as she had her husband. She said that he was a "giant man," 6 ft 5 inches tall, and full Cherokee. In reality, William A. Callaway was a normal-sized man of English (and possibly some Cherokee) stock. When he was 18, he married a 21-year-old neighbor, Mary Garrett "Polly" Sexton [144]. Mary was the daughter of Robert Sexton and his wife Nancy Driskill Sexton. Robert and Nancy were both the children of Revolutionary War veterans—Solomon Sexton in Georgia, and George Driskill in Maryland. Robert and Nancy Sexton were living on 240 acres on Walnut Fork in Jackson County, Georgia as early as 1823 in an area that would later become a part of Hall County.

Granny Dollar had two elder sisters who survived infancy.

Her eldest sister, Matilda Minerva Callaway, married William Thomas Christian in April 1863, and her other surviving elder sister Mary Elizabeth Callaway, married James Elijah Ragen in August 1861, leaving Nancy as the eldest child living at home by the age of 15. At this time her mother had, in addition to Nancy, six younger children to look after, while her father, William was away, first fighting in the Civil War, and then working in the mines of north Georgia. Nancy grew up, according to Callaway family researchers, on a farm near (or adjacent to) that of her grandfather John Callaway.

When the Civil War started, Nancy was 13 years old. Her father volunteered for the Forsyth and Gwinnett "Home Guard Volunteers," a home guard unit formally designated as Company F, 6th Regiment, 1st Brigade, 1st Division of the Georgia State Troops. Georgia's home guard units were loosely organized, local militias that worked in coordination with the Confederate Army. They were charged primarily with the defense of the home front, as well as tracking down Confederate Army deserters. Home guard units were almost exclusively made up of older men and other men exempt from service in the Confederate Army. Nancy Callaway's future husband, Nelson Dollar Jr., would also serve in the home guard unit at the same time as William A. Callaway. But, he would enlist in the regular army following his home guard service. Nelson Dollar's father "Nelse," 62 years old at the beginning of the war, also served with William A. Callaway in the home guard.

William A. Callaway did not die in the battle of Atlanta, as Nancy claimed, but survived his six-month enlistment to return, for a short while, to his family at Sugar Hill. By the end of the war, William had a second "commitment" about 30 miles northwest in Cherokee County, Georgia. At almost 40 years of age, he had met and became involved in a relationship with a 25-year-old, single woman named Catherine Eliza Brown. Catherine was the daughter of Joshua Brown, a native of Buncombe County, North Carolina, who was living in Gwinnett County by 1830, but who had migrated into Cherokee County by 1840. According to Callaway family tradition: One day, William hooked up two mules to a buckboard wagon and, with what cash he had on hand, drove away, leaving what little the war had spared the family to Mary and her eleven surviving children.

When Nancy's grandfather, John Callaway, died in 1891, he left a will in which he stated: "If my son be [is] alive at this time, he gets my land." He had no way of knowing that he would outlive his son William by almost four years. At the death of William's mother Elizabeth, in 1898, Mary and her children would inherit all of her father-in-law's land, stock, and possessions. By the time his will was probated, and his heirs distributed the proceeds, each (including Nancy) inherited a 1/10th share of his entire estate[145].

Nancy Callaway's mother, Mary Garrett Sexton, was born in January 1823[146] in Jackson County, Georgia. After William left her and their family, Mary continued to live in Gwinnett County until April 1900, when the estate of her mother-in-law, who passed away in 1898, was finally probated. Mary then followed the lead of some of her children and moved to Blount County, Alabama, near the town of Liberty. She was enumerated in the 1900 US Census in Blount County along with her daughter, Francis Callaway, and her granddaughter (the orphaned daughter of her son George Augustus Callaway), Mary E. Callaway. In January 1901 Mary died at the age of 79 in Blount County, less than a year after her move to Alabama.

"My brothers and sisters are all dead"

Mary and William had twelve children in the 20 years they were together, the last born in March 1865 near the end of the Civil War. Their oldest, Matilda Minerva Callaway[147], was born in Gwinnett County in December 1845, when her father William was 20 years old and her mother was 23. Matilda married a carpenter, William Thomas Christian, in Gwinnett County on April 26, 1863. They had only one child, a daughter, Senia Lucinda Christian, in 1864. Matilda died at the Georgia State Sanitarium in 1926.

William and Mary's second and third children were twin daughters, Mary Elizabeth Callaway[148] and Emeline Garrison Callaway. They were born in 1846. Emeline was named after her mother's sister, Charity Emeline Sexton. Emeline would not live long, and the Callaways would reuse the name Emeline as Nancy's middle name two years later. Mary Elizabeth Callaway married James Elijah Ragen in Gwinnett County on August 20, 1861, when she was 15 years old. She died (probably in childbirth) in 1865 at 19 with no surviving children.

In 1848, Mary Callaway gave birth to her fourth daughter, Nancy Emeline Callaway[149] who would become known as

Granny Dollar. Almost two years after Nancy was born, in March 1850, Mary would deliver her first boy, John Albert Callaway, named for his paternal grandfather. John married Mary Jane Higgens in Gwinnett County on June 7, 1875. John Albert and his family moved to Blount County, Alabama, to be followed later by their mother and many other siblings, around 1891. John died in Blount County in 1927.

Three years later, in 1853, the Callaways began another string of four girls, starting with Sarah Missouri[150], in October 1853. Sarah married George W. Sanders on November 15, 1875, in Elbert County, Georgia. Sarah and her husband were among the first of the Callaway siblings to move to Blount County, Alabama, arriving there in the mid-1880s. She died there in 1934. Next was Frances L. Callaway[151], born in June 1854. Frances never married. She moved to Blount County, Alabama, with her mother and lived there until her death in 1937.

Then there was California Savannah Callaway, born in January 1858. California married William Thomas Johnson in 1878 in Gwinnett County. Records show that the Johnsons moved to Fischer's Mill, DeKalb County around 1899[152]. By 1901, records indicate they were in the Saint Elmo community of Chattanooga, Hamilton County, Tennessee, where California died in 1936.

Georgia Ann Callaway, born in February 1860, married Thomas C. White on February 17, 1881. By 1900, Georgia Ann was a widow living in Teloga with a man named Chelsey Cross. Teloga is a small community in Chattanooga Valley near Menlo, Georgia, about 20 miles northeast of River Park, where Granny Dollar lived. Georgia Ann later married Chelsey Cross in June 1902 in Chattooga County. Records show that by 1910, Georgia Ann Callaway Cross lived in Alpine, Georgia, in Broomtown Valley about 12 miles from River Park, Alabama. In 1914, Georgia Ann was married, yet again, to a man named Calvin Cordell. In 1920, they lived among the rest of her siblings in Liberty, Blount County, Alabama, where she died in 1940.

In March 1861, William's namesake, William Asbury Callaway,[153] was born, the second son and 10th child of William and Mary Callaway. William Asbury would be the first of three sons and the last born before the Civil War. He married Malinda Jane Lafon in Gwinnett County, Georgia, in January 1882, and they moved to Blount County, Alabama, before 1900.

William and Mary Callaway's eleventh child, George Agustus "Gus" Callaway[154], was born in 1864. He married Nancy Leugenia "Janey" Monday in January 1888 in Gwinnett County, Georgia. Records show he died before 1900.

Finally, the last child born to William and Mary was James Noah Callaway, born on March 4, 1865, and named after his great uncle Noah Driskill[155]. Noah married Martha Allie Costine around 1893 and died in Mitchell County, Texas, in 1952.

While James Noah Callaway was the last of Mary Sexton Callaway's children, born when she was 43 years old, he was not the last of William Callaway's children. Near the end of the Civil War[156], in the spring of 1865, William hitched up a wagon with two mules, and, taking what little money and possessions he had on him, drove away. His ultimate destination was the little community of Canada Creek, near present-day Suches, Union County, Georgia. His focus, the 24-year-old daughter of Joshua and Catherine Brown, would soon give birth to William's thirteenth child, a daughter Milly D. Callaway (b. January 1867). Milly married William Michael Waters around 1893 in Lumpkin County, Georgia. She died in 1941.

Texanna (or Texie Ann) Callaway was born in April 1868. She married Stephen A. "Stevie" Palmer in 1885 in Union County, Georgia. The Palmers were in Sale Creek, Hamilton County, Tennessee, by 1900, and she died around 1900.

William S. "Will" Callaway was born in 1869. He married Eldorado Jane "Ellie" Waters in 1886 in Lumpkin County, Georgia. Will Callaway died in 1899 in Nimblewill, Lumpkin County, Georgia.

Ulysses C. "Ule" Callaway was born in 1871 and is believed to have died before 1899.

Thomas Lee Callaway, born in 1873, married Susan Seabolt in 1890 in Union County, Georgia, and died in 1913.

Maggie Elizabeth Callaway was born in 1875. She married William M. Newberry in 1892 in Union County, Georgia, and died in 1939 in Gordon County, Georgia.

Born in 1877 in Union County, Georgia, John Joseph Callaway married Rachel Wehunt in Union County, Georgia, 1n 1892.

She died in 1896, and John Joseph remarried Evalina "Ava" Gamblin in 1896. John Joseph died in 1955 in Georgia.

Finally, their last child, Hyram Callaway, was born in Canada, Union County, Georgia, in 1879. Not much is known about Hyram Callaway. He may have died young.

Nancy Dollar said, in 1928, "that all of her brothers and sisters were dead." However, at the time, at least six of her 11 siblings and three of her eight half-siblings survived. Nancy was estranged from her family and had no known contact with them. Certainly, there are no reliable mentions of them. None lived in DeKalb County after 1901, and none are known to have attended Nancy's funeral. Local legends identify Joe Callahan as a brother of Nancy. However, there is no indication of a Joe Callahan in DeKalb County, Alabama, during this time. Also, the name "Callahan" appears to have been an invention of Nancy's. None of her siblings or half-siblings adopted any other name but their own. In fact, Nancy's half-siblings and their mother adopted Callaway's name [157], even though she was never married to William and her legal name remained Brown. The source of this information is likely Nancy herself since she did have a half-brother called "Joe" (John Joseph Callaway), and Nancy is the only one to have referred to her family by the name of Callahan. Two of Granny Dollar's sisters lived within 20 miles of her in 1900, but, by 1923, they had long since moved away when she first appeared at the Master School.

"My father was a big man"

Confederate Artillery began shelling Fort Sumter, in the harbor of Charleston, South Carolina, in the pre-dawn hours of April 12, 1861. Union guns responded. The Civil War had begun. For the rest of the spring and into the summer of 1861, hundreds of thousands of men, assuming the war would be long over by Christmas, volunteered for a short term of military service. As many as half of them signed on for a one-year term. As the conflict extended into the winter of 1861, the South readied their army for a more prolonged fight. But men who had already served six months or more needed to return to their farms and families. The excitement and patriotic zeal of the moment had waned and the prospect of a long bloody war was now a reality.

When Fort Sumter was shelled, William A. Callaway was 35 years old and would turn 36 within one month. Records show he was not among the volunteers known as the "men of '61." He waited until October of that year to join, and he would not join the regular army, as did younger men, but the Home Guard, a Georgia militia unit intended for older men. As was common practice across the Confederacy, the states held older men in reserve and allowed them to join state militias rather than the regular army while waiting. They used the home guard units primarily to guard their home territory and pursue and capture Confederate deserters. The Confederate government worried about their ability to raise an army and felt that the proper policy was to appeal to patriotism. By early 1862, no volunteers were filling the decimated regiments. The terms of enlistments for almost half the army neared its close in April 1862, and citizens met the frantic appeals of confederate journals and newspapers with stiff indifference. This resulted in the more vocal of the rebellion's leaders focusing their sights on conscription as a necessary step to restore the hope of the young Confederacy.

In early April 1862, the Confederate forces of General Albert Sidney Johnston's Army of Mississippi met the Union's Army of Tennessee, led by General Ulysses S. Grant at Pittsburg Landing in Hardin County in western Tennessee. By the second day of fighting, Johnston's second-in-command, General P. G. T. Beauregard (who had taken command after Johnston's battlefield death), realizing that he was low on ammunition and food, withdrew beyond Shiloh Church. By 5 pm, when their covering force had withdrawn, the Confederate Army had lost over 10,500 men, dead, wounded, or missing. Nine days later, the Confederate government would pass the first Conscription Act, making three years of service in the Confederate Army mandatory for all men between the ages of 18 and 35. The Governor of Georgia immediately turned all state troops over to the regular army, and all men who were currently serving had 24 months added to their enlistment. But, just as Nelson Dollar was transferring from the home guard to the regular army, William Callaway was leaving service. His six-month term of enlistment in the state troops ended. He was 36 years old, missing 24 months of mandatory service by a few days.

Although William would have likely joined the state troops as a strategy to avoid army service, he had been fortunate in the timing. However, his luck would not hold for long. On September 27, 1862, Congress would extend the exemption age for men to 45 years. However, they expressly exempted iron mine workers since their product was much-needed by the army. Iron ore mining in Georgia began around 1840 with a blast furnace being erected on Stamp Creek in Bartow County. By 1853, five such furnaces were in operation in that county. Many mines were operating in the area and in the mountains to the east to feed the furnaces. William had stayed at home for a time after returning from his home guard service. He was eligible and obligated to serve a three-year term; at the very least, he was subject to recall, serving an additional 24 months. With few choices in front of him, sometime, probably around the fall of 1862, William headed for one of the iron mining operations near Canton, Georgia, in nearby Cherokee County about 30 miles from Sugar Hill.

In the years before the Civil War, north Georgia had a booming mining industry. There was a concentration of iron mining and smelting in Bartow and Cherokee Counties along Stamp Creek and the Etowah River, near present-day Lake Allatoona. These iron-rich areas stretched west to Pine Log Mountain and Waleska in Cherokee County. Along what is known today as the Cartersville and Emerson faults, the hills were rich in iron. Throughout the 1800s, iron from these areas was commonly used throughout Georgia to supply implements principally for farm use and rail lines. But, the increased need, just before and during the Civil War, for iron for armaments and mechanized equipment, meant that the iron mining business in Georgia, and all the Confederacy, was a critical infrastructure and, therefore, workers in iron mining, at least in Georgia, were expressly exempted from conscription.

The idea of becoming an iron miner, or smelter, was neither original nor isolated to William Callaway. The Donaldson's Furnace, on Shoal Creek about five miles west of Canton, was constructed sometime around this time by Judge Joseph Donaldson, a Justice of the Inferior Court of Cherokee County and a large slave owner. Donaldson, eager to keep his sons free from conscription into the army, bought a lot of forfeited property in a Sheriff's sale and built an iron smelting furnace, putting all of his sons to work in the mining industry. Interestingly, the Donaldson furnace was never fired, and there was no evidence of iron or slag found in the area. It is equally unclear whether William Callaway ever worked in the iron mines or at the furnaces, or if he hid out in the mountains among the ironworks.

By 1860, Joshua Brown was living with his family, including his 20-year-old daughter Catherine, near the Chester mine in militia district 818 (called Mullins) in Cherokee County. Mullins and the communities of Orange and Lathemtown were on the main road from the Sugar Hill/Cumming area to Canton, the county seat of Cherokee County. It would have taken William about four hours to travel, by horseback, between his home and Mullins. History does not record how, or exactly when, William met Joshua's young, single daughter Catherine, but it was likely during this time and in this area. William would continue to work in north Georgia and travel home to Gwinnett occasionally until the war was almost over. At that point, he no longer needed to live in the remote mountains to avoid conscription.

By March 1865, it was apparent to all but the most die-hard Confederates that the South was losing the war. There would no longer be any reason for William to work in the remote mountains, and he could safely, and legally, return to farming on his Gwinnett County estate. Although Mary had given birth to her last child on the 4th day of that month, William would not return to his family. On March 29, 1865, just eleven days before the Confederacy's formal surrender at Appomattox Courthouse, William filed papers[158] in Gwinnett County transferring all of his property to his wife Mary Callaway and their children. Nine months later, in January 1866, Catherine Brown gave birth to her first child, Milly D. Callaway[159].

"...and soon they are dead"

By the mid-1880s, the departure, and continuing notoriety, of William A. Callaway had humiliated Mary Garrett Callaway and her children since he left the family more than 20 years before. In that time, Callaway and Catherine had been raising an additional eight Callaway children, five boys and three girls. The Callaway clan of Union County, Georgia, was well known both in those remote parts, as well as in the newspapers of Gwinnett and Atlanta as thieves and bullies. Each time a news article appeared, the editors took care to remind people that William had another wife and family living in Gwinnett. The people that settled the gold and iron mining regions of north Georgia were of all sorts. But, on average, they were a rough, shiftless, fighting lot. The Callaways fit right in. Although the region wasn't completely lawless, the law was slow to move; and in these remote mountains, people were reluctant to pursue justice too swiftly for fear of retaliation. Thus, the Callaway boys were raised to take what they wanted.

Around this time, John Cannon, a wholesale grocer in Dahlonega, Georgia, had an idea to increase the business at his store and bring groceries, dry goods, and hardware from outside the Canada District to its citizens. He persuaded Bill Davis, who had opened a retail store at Suches (*pronounced SUCH-iss*), to send an application to the US Postal Service and request that he be allowed to open a post office in the new store. The Suches Post Office opened on March 6, 1886. Suches was a high mountain community in the upper mountainous reaches of southwestern Union County. This upper "valley above the clouds" was cradled below the outer eastern line of the Blue Ridge Range. It was named after an Indian chieftain who once lived in the valley near the Bill Davis store site. John Cannon himself was the first postmaster of the Post Office there. But, it was his wife that "kept" the Post Office.

In February of 1887, two white men broke into the Suches Post Office, taking a safe, some cash, and a large number of stamps. A posse, suspecting the two eldest Callaway boys, went to the home of their father, William A. Callaway, and, searching, identified a package of stamped envelopes that had been taken in the robbery along with other items that indicated that the Callaways were, in fact, the guilty parties. Deputy Marshal James Harbison, assisted by Dennis Griswell, decided to arrest the suspects without taking time to gather a posse. The two deputies were soon facing the boys' father, William, and his revolver. Within a minute, four of the Callaway boys arrived, 18-year-old Will, 16-year-old "Ule," 14-year-old Lee, and 10-year-old Joe. After William ordered his sons to go inside and arm themselves, Dennis Griswell bravely stepped between the four boys and the doorway to their house, locking the hammer on his revolver. The standoff lasted several tense minutes as Harbison attempted to talk the "old man" into putting his weapon away. Just when things seemed to be quieting down, William's wife Catherine stepped out of the house waving an ancient "cap and ball" revolver and threatening to shoot anyone who "laid a hand" on her husband. Deputies patiently explained that they had no intention of arresting the older man, but were there to arrest the boys, and she and William agreed to put down their guns. The deputies left with two of the Callaway boys, Will and "Ule," [160] closely followed by their father and mother and a large group of relatives, who were determined to follow them to Dahlonega to make sure that everything was "done up right."

Federal Marshals transported the boys from Dahlonega to Atlanta, where they held them in jail for several months. Under federal law, a court could find a defendant incompetent to stand trial if he was unable to understand the nature and consequences of his crime or the proceedings against him and was, therefore, unable to assist properly in his defense. In modern days, in such a case, he is involuntarily committed until his competency is restored, and he may be indefinitely held, but, in Georgia in the 1880s, the system was not quite so effective at keeping track of people. Although the federal court system in 1887 did not have a separate concept for prosecuting minors, some jurisdictions tended to be more liberal and let juveniles off with a stern warning. After several months in jail, the Callaway boys were examined by physicians, who certified both to be "idiots." The court then released them to return to their lawless ways in north Georgia.

Perhaps it was William A. Callaway's behavior in handling the arrest of his boys, his general demeanor in the community, or a possible coincidence. But, in late June of the same year, a mere two months after the robbery at Suches, a Union County Grand Jury returned a true bill charging William A. Callaway with bigamy.[161] True bills for state charges were also returned against the two young Callaway boys for burglary of the post office.[162] Deputy Sheriff Marion Williams obtained warrants for the arrest of the three. Unfortunately, a small town could not conceal such an action, and the Callaway men soon learned of the existence of the warrants and the Sheriff's plan. William responded by swearing that he would never be arrested and that he would kill any officer, and anyone else, who attempted to arrest them. Neighbors tried to reason with him and convince him to leave the county rather than confronting the deputies. William responded that he was prepared for a fight and would kill five of any crowd who attempted to arrest him. On June 22, 1887, as he prepared to go to work in the fields, his wife, Catherine Callaway, begged William to either surrender himself or leave his guns at home. William told his wife to get his burial clothes ready and departed for the fields, armed with a pistol, a rifle, and a shotgun.

Williams assembled a posse of six men[163]: George Gurley, John Nelson, George Clarke, Thomas Lunsford, William Seabolt, and Fulton Williams. When they arrived in the Callaway farm's vicinity, Deputy Williams and his brother Fulton, finding William Callaway isolated, moved slowly to get within 25 yards of him and called out to him to surrender. Callaway instantly pulled his revolver and attempted to fire at the deputies, but his weapon misfired. As William began to flee, Marion Williams called to him to halt and implored him to "talk things over." Callaway continued to run, taking cover behind a large stump, and began to fire his revolver furiously at Williams. In the meantime, two of the Callaway boys saw what was happening and left their plows in the field to run to their father's aid. One of the boys picked up a rifle and joined his father in firing at the deputies. George Gurley tackled the other Callaway son before he could reach a weapon. William Callaway, seeing this, picked up a double-barreled shotgun and leveled it at Gurley. At this point, the entire posse fired at the older man simultaneously, and he dropped to the ground, riddled with bullets. The remaining Callaway son continued to fire on the posse, with them returning the fire until he was wounded. Gurley, who had let loose of the other Callaway brother, when he began firing at William, watched helplessly, and the two Callaway boys escaped into the tree line.

William Callaway lived for about 30 minutes before succumbing to the 27 gunshot wounds he suffered. He had been true to his word, concerning not being arrested, but he had failed to kill, or even wound, any of the deputies. The long, checkered life of William A. Callaway had come to an inglorious end. He was 62 years old. It would mean another round of newspaper articles and behind-the-back whispers for Mary Garret Callaway and her children. William's purported widow, Catherine Callaway, would soon remarry, to John Wehunt, from nearby Nimblewill in Lumpkin County. But, for the Callaway boys, for a while, it would be business as usual.[164]

* * *

Soon after William Callaway's death and the pursuit, arrest, and release of the Callaway "idiots," the citizens of Union County began to get serious about their crime problem.

Federal prosecutors empaneled grand juries to take on the bullies and bootleggers that ran rampant across the territory. One by one, they held criminals responsible, taking down the "copper god worshipers[165]." During the summer of 1889, grand juries indicted several men who were arrested and taken to Atlanta to stand trial. One of the sons of William A. Callaway (while uncertain, it was likely Ulysses Callaway) was called upon to serve as a witness for the state at several trials. However, since the federal Judge in Atlanta had already accepted that Callaway was an "idiot," he could not testify. One by one, each of the cases was dismissed since the prosecutors had no other witnesses. On returning to the mountains of Union County in June 1889, Ule Callaway was cornered by his neighbors and severely flogged such that it was believed at the time that he would not recover"[166]. Ulysses Callaway does not appear in later records, while his brother William continued to live in the area. Therefore, it is likely "Ule" did not recover from this assault and died in 1889 at the age of 18.

****

With the smoke and gloom of the battles and riots seemingly passing away, the congregates at the Lebanon Church in Canada Valley were settling down to worship on a cold Sunday morning in November 1893, when Michael Waters (the husband of Granny Dollar's half-sister Milly Callaway) moved to the front of the church to make a statement. With hat in hand, a sorrowful Waters confessed that the week before, he had "mortally wounded" his brother-in-law, Will Callaway, at Lige Seabolt's[167] house in Coosa District. With only one side of the story being told, and with the target of the shooting being a Callaway, who the people of the county had deemed "a fair specimen of his father," the members of Lebanon Church were in complete sympathy with Waters. Waters explained that Will Callaway came to his house while he was away and, after securing all the guns in the home, robbed Water's young daughter of about $20 in household items along with all the Waters' ammunition. Callaway then started toward Blairsville, attempting to sell the items he had stolen. When he arrived at the Seabolt home he was joined by Michael Waters, who was with Deputy Sheriff Wash Woody[168] and Mr. Clemens. Will Callaway immediately began to fire on the three with his pistol. Michael Waters met him with a double-barrelled shotgun blast. The fight was over. Callaway gasped, "Mike, you've killed me." Michael Waters was careful to explain to the congregation how he inquired into the state of Callaway's salvation as he stood over him with the shotgun, saying, "pray to God for his pardoning grace!" But, in more ways than one, this would be a wasted effort. This incident would not mark the end of Will Callaway. He would barely pull through and continue his lawless ways across Union County.

* * *

Six years later, on Thursday, September 28, 1899, Constable J. F. Purdue arrived in Dahlonega, Georgia, with a prisoner in tow. The Sheriff was out of town, so Purdue locked up his prisoner to await the Coroner, John W. Satterfield's, return in the next day or two with the paperwork associated with the case. Satterfield had waited back a couple of days to assemble a jury to investigate a killing and arrive at a verdict. When they saw the prisoner, the people of Dahlonega just "put it up to another Callaway murder." He was 24-year-old Joe Callaway who had been hauled in from his home 11 miles west of Dahlonega, in the community of Nimblewill. Callaway would sit in jail for two days, awaiting the coroner's jury findings. Coroner Satterfield had been called out to investigate a grizzly scene.

Around sundown on Wednesday, Joe killed his brother Will Callaway with an ax. Will had come to his mother's house in Nimblewill to complain he had been cheated out of his estate settlement share. She sent him to the field to speak to his brother Joe, who was clearing some land "a good distance" from the house. No one was there to witness the killing, but six people testified to hearing a revolver shot. The sound of the shot sent several people running to find Will Callaway lying on the ground with two large ax wounds on his head and "his brains spilling onto the ground." One wound was on the right side of his forehead and the other on the back of his head. The wound on the back of the head appeared to have been made with the poll (or back) of the ax. Joe Callaway was still holding the murder weapon when witnesses arrived. A revolver lay nearby with one empty chamber. The finding of the Satterfield Coroner's Jury was self-defense. The life of another Callaway had come to an undignified end. This time, at the hand of his brother. On Saturday, Joe Callaway was released to return to his home.

* * *

"I'm coming to see you every day."

One of Granny Dollar's neighbors, on Lookout Mountain in the early 1920s, was Lafayette Morgan Lowman. Lowman, born March 22, 1863, in the mountainous area of Dawson County, Georgia, was the first child of Paton Monroe Lowman[169] and his wife, Sarah Bearden. By 1919, Morgan Lowman was a widower living in the Phillips area of Lookout Mountain. Morgan Lowman's father, Paton, was a hard-living man who had stood in the court docks in northwest Georgia more than a dozen times, mostly for illegal distilling. In January 1890, at the age of 60, Paton Lowman stood on a walkway outside of a Dawson County jail after being temporarily released to travel to Birmingham, Alabama, to attend the murder trial of his son, James Martin "Jace" Lowman. Paton told reporters gathered there that he was an innocent man, his son "Jace" was an innocent man, and that all of the Lowmans were innocent men.

"Jace" Lowman had been accused of killing Thomas Hudspeth during a Birmingham, Alabama bar fight. According to witnesses, Hudspeth, a 24-year-old Sharon, Pennsylvania, ironworker, was only a spectator to the fight and was simply in the wrong place at the wrong time. As witnesses reported,

Lowman stabbed Hudspeth through the heart, killing him instantly. He left a wife and two children. "Jace" Lowman escaped a murder conviction and returned to Dawson County, Georgia, only to be stabbed to death by an unknown assailant on May 20, 1894, on a lonely dark road in Gilmer County, near Ellijay, Georgia. Twenty-five years later, "Jace" Lowman's brother Benjamin Hill Lowman was found dead on another lonely dark Gilmer County road. Neither of these crimes was ever solved. Such was the hard life of the 'innocent' Lowman clan.

In July 1899, several Dawson County men gathered, as was their custom, to work on the rural roads in the upper part of the county. Paton Lowman's brother, Jefferson Morgan "Morge" Lowman, was among them. He had been drinking, and there was tension between him and his brother-in-law Benjamin Anderson, This tension probably arose from their joint moonshining activity, but there was no active fight between them. "Morge" Lowman simply raised a shovel and struck Anderson unexpectedly on the forehead, crushing it. Anderson fell in a heap with a groan, and Lowman continued to strike him on the head with the shovel two more times. Anderson died there on the road.

Lowman fled the scene, quickly pursued by a sheriff's posse. He was eventually captured in Gilmer County, Georgia, about six miles from the site of the killing. Even though several of Anderson's sons and his brother, John, were among the Sheriff's posse, Lowman made it safely to jail without being lynched—a most likely outcome in the northern mountains of Georgia at that time.

In mid-August 1899, 'Morge' Lowman stood trial before Judge J. B. Estes in Dawson County. After being convicted, [170] he was sentenced to hang in early October. However, 'Morge' appealed his verdict, unsuccessfully at first, to an appeals court in Habersham County, Georgia. He then went to the Georgia Supreme Court, where he won a new trial. For the second trial, all parties agreed that Lowman would plead guilty in return for a life sentence in prison, which he soon began to serve. In 1909, after a prison commission rejected his plea for release, and after having served barely 10 years for the brutal murder, Governor M. Hoke Smith of Georgia pardoned Lowman; This was the Governor's last official act, performed at 2:00 am of his last official day in office. 'Morge' Lowman moved back to neighboring Gilmer County, Georgia, and eventually died in Ellijay, Georgia, in 1929, thirty years after escaping the death sentence and twenty years after being freed from his life sentence. Most of the Lowman clan men lived hard lives, but they were experienced with the law and exceptional at gaining their freedom. In most situations, they used their freedom to return to their lawless ways.

On November 18, 1909, around the same time 'Morge' Lowman was released from prison, his nephew, Lafayette Morgan Lowman, who was convicted in Alabama, with his son Joe, for illegal distilling, was incarcerated in the Federal Prison in Atlanta. He was released on January 15, 1911, after serving an 18-month sentence and paying a $100 fine. This branch of the Lowman clan had been living in Jackson County, Alabama near Pisgah since just after the turn of the century[171]. Soon after his release, the younger Morgan Lowman returned to Alabama, settling in DeKalb County on Brow Road in the community of Phillips about a mile from the rented home of Nelson and Granny Dollar.

The Lowmans and the Dollars were living about five miles north of Mentone on the West Fork of the Little River, near the Georgia state line. Another family that was living near them was that of the Abbots.[172] First-time mother, 17-year-old Clara Augusta Sharp Abbot was the daughter of Florence Flarity and Calvin Martin Sharp, a Lookout Mountain farmer. Calvin Sharp died in 1920, and Florence married Calvin's brother William Pearl Sharp. At that time, Pearl and Florence Sharp were living in Chattanooga Valley, to the East of Lookout Mountain, at Cedar Grove in Walker County, Georgia. Clara's husband was 23-year-old William Samuel Abbot, the son of John F. Abbot and Mary Smith of Lookout Mountain. William Samuel Abbot and Clara Sharp Abbot's first son, Floyd Harold Abbot, was born on April 18, 1919. When it was time for Floyd to arrive, in addition to being Good Friday, it was very late in the evening, and the doctor from Valley Head was unable to get his horse and buggy up the mountain in time for the birth. With no doctor on hand, Granny looked after Clara during Floyd's birth and immediately afterward, although it was likely illegal by this time.[173] After the birth of Floyd, the Abbots continued to live near the Dollars and the families were close.

In September 1920, when the baby was 17 months old, the young Abbot family's life was shattered. As their families gathered, probably to work on the fall harvesting, 24-year-old William Samuel Abbot was mercilessly beaten to death by his violent and notorious neighbor Morgan Lowman[174] as they quarreled while attempting to start an automobile in the road a short distance from the Abbot home. In a scene reminiscent of that of his Uncle "Morge," Morgan Lowman stood in the road and struck Abbot at least five times with a seasoned oak walking stick. The Abbot family carried the senseless William back to their home and attempted to care for him. No doctor was called, and it is impossible to say whether Granny Dollar was called to provide care. But the Alabama Supreme Court later speculated that Abbot "might have recovered with the exercise of more prudence and with better nurses."[175] Abbot died about eight hours later.

Lowman was convicted of second-degree manslaughter and sentenced to eight years in prison. Abbot's young widow and one-year-old Frank soon moved to Battelle, in Wills Valley to live with her parents[176], the Sharps. Soon after she moved, Clara gave birth, on December 1st of that same year, to William Abbot's second child, a daughter Willie Mae Abbot. Granny Dollar may have delivered this baby as well. She certainly looked in on, and cared for, Clara during the pregnancy. While Battelle was about 12 miles by road, from the Dollar home, it was less than two miles "as the crow flies." Granny Dollar made numerous visits to the young mother's home by walking up and down a steep, 2-mile footpath near Crow Gap to the valley and back to the top of the mountain. According to Floyd Abbot, Granny would continually beg Clara, during these visits, to bring "little Floyd" and visit her and Nelson back up on the mountain. So, once she had recovered from her latest pregnancy, they went with Clara carrying Floyd up Granny's mountain footpath. They spent the night with the Dollar couple in their little cabin.[177] In the eyes of many outsiders, granny women like Granny Dollar, were, at best, superstitious and illiterate nuisances. At worst, they represented dangerous frauds. But to the families they served, they were cherished friends, true neighbors, and caring healthcare providers.

An article appeared in the March 23, 1950 issue of Scottsboro, Alabama newspaper, The Progressive Age, celebrating the 100th birthday of Lafayette Morgan Lowman; the paper listed Lowman as having been born on March 22, 1850. According to the article, Morgan Lowman came to Jackson County, Alabama, from Dawson County, Georgia around 1900. Dawsonville is only about 12 miles south of Nimblewill, Georgia where Nancy Dollar's half-siblings lived in the 1890s. Although Lowman admitted to living a hard life, no mention was made of the six years he spent in an Alabama prison for the killing of William Abbot. There is also no mention of his, or his family's, other troubles with the law. Lowman "clearly recalled" his father joining the Confederate Army and "recalled" going with his father when he was first mustered into service. However, Morgan Lowman was actually born in March 1862, one year to the month after his father mustered into service.

Following this celebrated "100-year" birthday, Lowman lived another two years and three months, passing away on June 17, 1952. His gravestone and his obituary in *the Fort Payne Journal*, gave his age at death as 102. Like Nancy Dollar, however, his age had been greatly exaggerated. When he died in Jackson County, in 1952, Lafayette Morgan Lowman was 88 years old.

"Folks comes and helps me, but I'm tired now"

Milford Howard believed that Granny Dollar would live to be 160 years old, as she often claimed she would do, if it were not for winters. Granny was the busiest person he had ever known. In December 1929, Granny sent word to Howard that she was looking forward to the spring and intended to plant a new orchard to replace her failing fruit trees. When told that she would never live to see the new trees bear fruit, Granny laughed optimistically. Howard believed that the secret of Granny's longevity lay in physical activity. According to Howard, she lived every day as a great adventure. He predicted that when Granny died, it would be in winter when she was shut in by bad weather and had little to do.

In December 1930, one year after planning her new fruit orchard, Granny Dollar lay in her little cabin near death from congestive heart failure. Kind neighbors, many as poor as she, kept vigil with her, unwilling that she should be left alone. One day, when Dee Gilliam, and his two sons, stopped by to look in on her, she guided him to one of the three trunks she kept and asked him to count her money. Gilliam removed a bundle of bills carefully wrapped in blue paper and counted 23 dollars. Granny asked Dee to make sure that the money be used to buy a headstone for her grave. Dee swore to do so. Among other last requests was one she made to Floyd Cordell.[178] Granny asked Floyd to make sure that an Indian funerary dance was performed at her burial service. Cherokee funerary rites are complex and often include a solemn dance. She asked that they dance around her corpse in her cabin after she passed away.

Near midnight on January 18, 1931, Nancy Emeline Callaway "Granny" Dollar passed away. After the furniture was cleared from her room, a funerary dance was conducted, and plans were made to bury her. Neighbors Joseph Cordell, his son,[179] and David Keith[180] built an oak coffin for Granny. Milford Howard persuaded DeKalb County officials to contribute $5 to cover the cost of a hearse to carry her body to the cemetery. Days later, about 75 people gathered at Little River Baptist Church for her funeral service. Pallbearers included Ed Gilliam,[181] Floyd Cordell, and David Keith. Milford Howard spoke at the funeral, Reverend J. M. White[182] delivered the eulogy, and Frances Kerby[183] sang. Following the ceremony, Granny was laid to rest in the tiny church's cemetery beside her husband Nelson, who had died eight years before. It was a cold, rainy day. Although Granny had ensured that Nelson's grave had a tombstone, her own would not have a marker for several years. Greedy neighbors, who had heard rumors that Granny kept money hidden in her cabin, broke in after her death and stole the $23 intended for her tombstone.

The January 28, 1931 issue of *the Fort Payne Journal* paid tribute to Nancy Dollar as the "oldest citizen in the county." Milford

Howard repeated the story of her being the daughter of a Cherokee father and a "beautiful" white woman. Howard described her last few weeks at River Park as a glorious time with Granny being visited and attended day and night by friends and neighbors. In her last minute, he said, she clapped her hands together "while a look of rapture lighted up her wonderful old face." Howard said that she was "a true warrior that fought life's battles bravely and well."

****

Years later, on May 26, 1961, Girl Scout troop 24 of Fort Payne, took over the Boy Scout cabin on Lookout Mountain for the Memorial Day weekend. Bubbling over with energy, the girls decided to hike down to Little River to identify as many flowers as possible. That night, they settled down around the fire for a meal, "smores, and story swapping." Among those were stories of the ghost of Granny Dollar. Afterward, the girls went on a moonlight hike. At every turn of the trail and in every shadow of every tree, they expected to see the ghost pop out. But, they were disappointed. Granny's ghost just would not cooperate. When they settled down to sleep that night, finally exhausted, squawks, squeaks, and the occasional flash of a flashlight kept them awake long into the night. Similar scenes have been repeated in the camps of Lookout Mountain for years. It isn't clear when the legend of Granny Dollar became the legend of Granny Dollar's ghost. But, given the abundance of boys and girls camps in the Lookout Mountain area, it is likely that it happened shortly after her death.

On December 29, 1977, the *Abbeville Herald* published a

story under the *Alabama Folkways* column, which set out Granny Dollar's tale and reported her as a full-fledged legend. The story repeated many of the inaccurate "facts" that were "known" about Granny. The story also sets out a few actual facts from the remembrances of people then living. The paper credited her with having a "vast knowledge" of herbal medicines and having done a great deal of granny-doctoring in the Lookout Mountain area. The writer, Henry Willet, said when he was about five or six years old, Granny Dollar asked his mother and father if she could take the young boy home with her. She loved children and had never had any of her own. When his father refused to let the youngster accompany her to her home, she threatened him with a "spell," saying she would have him carried off to an Indian reservation.

There were dozens of stories about Granny having money or treasure buried near her cabin; there was also evidence, as late as the 1970s, of digging in the vicinity. Most of these stories can be traced to Granny herself. The legend states that Granny knew where the Indians buried their treasure before their removal and that she had dug up some of their treasure and reburied it. She told hundreds of visitors stories about hidden Indian gold and where exactly to search for it. Milford Howard said, "Many a credulous person has gone on a wild goose chase hunting a treasure trove under Granny's direction." Howard stated that Granny even offered to tell him where to find enough treasure to fund the Master School. How such stories were taken seriously when their subject was an indigent elderly woman, is anyone's guess. After she was buried, no money was found among her possessions. Many people assumed that whatever money she possessed was stolen by one of her many visitors. Still, others presumed she had buried her "treasure." It was thought that she had hidden her husband's gold watch under a rock near the Little River. However, for those who lived in the area, "Granny's" ghost was said to appear near the ruins of her old cabin; on some nights, the far-away barking of her ghost dog Buster could be heard as well.

In May 1982, storyteller, author, folklorist, and journalist Kathryn Tucker Windham attended the Alabama Library Association Convention in Huntsville, Alabama, where she was honored as state chairman for National Library Week. Windham, who was born in Selma, Alabama, in 1918, worked for *The Birmingham News*. In 1969, Windham wrote *13 Alabama Ghosts, and Jeffrey,* a book of "true" ghost stories based on local folklore. Jeffrey was a purported ghost that took up residence in the Windham house in 1966. According to the letter printed in the foreword to the book, Windham became interested in ghost stories after her family heard footsteps in rooms that were later found to be empty. According to Windham, the family identified Jeffrey as a ghost haunting her family. Windham continued to publish follow-up works about ghosts for the next forty years. When she appeared at the 1982 Library Association Convention, she introduced a new set of ghost stories. Included in this set was the story of the "Ghost of Granny Dollar."

Windham said that when mourners returned from attending her burial at Little River Baptist Church cemetery, they were met by a growling Buster. Deciding on the spot that the dog could not live without Granny, they agreed to put him down and mercifully killed the dog. They laid him to rest at the foot of a giant boulder just behind her cabin. According to Windham, it was soon after the theft of her tombstone money that people first began to report seeing Granny Dollar and her dog, in the vicinity of her cabin. In 1973, Mrs. Annie Young, of Fort Payne, collected contributions to purchase a headstone. On January 31, 1973, the marker was placed at Granny's grave. Since that day, according to Windham's story, no one has seen "Granny." Her dog Buster is still occasionally heard to bark, as if he continues to guard something or someone he loves.

In November 2013, a group of friends working in DeSoto State Park went to explore the area of the river during their lunch break. On their way back to their camp, one of them saw an old woman with her dog. The woman did not speak to the group, and the group did not speak to the women. But, afterward, they realized that there was no way for the woman to have been there with no car parked nearby. Though they are not abnormal (or paranormal), such encounters continue to evoke eerie feelings among visitors and residents, and tales of the ghost of Granny Dollar continue to be told.

"Sit and 'bide."

Granny Dollar has continued to be a local celebrity and curiosity for more than 90 years, with our interest being driven, in part, by the otherness she represents. She is simultaneously the Indian we all wanted to be when growing up as well as the ancient warrior we all hope to be in our old age. But is this the reason we should care? And, is it the reason her neighbors cared during her lifetime?

Floyd Abbot described Granny as a nurturing midwife and friend who looked after his family's well-being when his mother was vulnerable. Folklorist Henry Willet wrote of the love that Granny showed for children. She was loved by the community, as evident in her neighbors being eager to care for her in the last years of her life. According to Milford Howard, Granny always had something from her garden, her orchards, or her farmyard to share with her neighbors. In fact, there is little sign that her contemporaries, except for those who wrote about her, took much interest in her "Indianness" or her extreme age. For readers who had never met Granny, these traits were just the hook that grabbed their attention. But, for those who knew her personally, there was little interest to be found in these aspects of her character. Milford Howard was reluctant to write about Granny, and for almost five years, he resisted. He became her benefactor, not because he hoped to exploit her story for gain, but simply because she was a neighbor who needed help.

During her lifetime and in the years immediately following it, Granny became known less for her age and ethnic heritage and more as a local curiosity who told fortunes among the summer visitors of Mentone. There is little doubt that in earlier years, she was equally known as a midwife and folk healer. Contemporary writers often questioned the integrity of her age claims. They placed the term "half-Indian" in quotation marks to indicate that it was her unverified claim rather than fact. Granny was recognized (and renowned) among her contemporaries for her actions rather than her status. In subsequent years, it was her age and her heritage (both highly exaggerated qualities) as well as the myths of her ghost that continued to capture the fascinated attention of readers and entrance listeners around the campfires of Lookout Mountain.

This book breaks through those myths and exaggerations and exposes the real identity of Granny Dollar. It sheds light on many of the exciting, though less known, features of her story. It also reveals the stories of several "normal" characters who inhabited Granny's life, such as Sadie Shrader, William Anderson Callaway, Lafayette Morgan Lowman, and many others. These, along with the better-known characters like Milford Howard and Winifred Black, each have their own stories to be told. If there is a challenge to emerge from this work, it is that we should all take on the responsibility to dig deeper into the stories we are told and collect and preserve the tidbits of history that we find there. The objective is not to expose a fictional story. Rather, the goal is to shed light on the real stories that hide *within* fiction.

"...to know them and their secret ways."

Was Granny Dollar's name Nancy Callahan, and was she the eldest child of William Callahan, a "full-blooded" Cherokee, and Mary Sexton, a mixed-blood Cherokee/Scots-Irish?

No quite. Granny Dollar was born Nancy Emeline Callaway (not Callahan). She was the fourth child of William Anderson Callaway (primarily of English descent, but possibly having Cherokee heritage through his mother) and Mary Garrett Sexton (primarily of Scots-Irish ancestry). Nancy's use of the name Callahan to obscure her true identity was intentional. It was likely used to shield herself from embarrassing details about her family, including the well-known and well-documented abandonment of her family by her father and his death at the hands of Georgia deputies, the lawless lives of her father and half-brothers, the killing of her half-brother by another half-brother, her family's disputes regarding the settlement of the estate of her grandfather, and other embarrassing events.

Was Granny Dollar really born in Buck's Pocket, Alabama, in 1822? Or was she born in July 1827 in

Forsyth County, Georgia?

Nancy Emeline Callahan was born in Gwinnett County, Georgia, in June 1848. She appears in the 1850 Census (2 years old), the 1860 Census (11 years old), and the 1880 Census (32 years old) in Gwinnett County, Georgia. All of these dates are consistent with a June (or July) 1848 birthdate. By 1900, Nancy had exaggerated her age by eight years. In 1910, she had exaggerated her age by 11 years, and by 1930, she had exaggerated her age by 13 years. Since Nancy was born in 1848, the 1910 and 1930 US Census could be influenced by "age-heaping" (the tendency to round an age up to the nearest 5 or 10 years), with an additional decade accidentally added. Meanwhile, by 1928, Howard was reporting her birth date as July 1827 (a 21-year exaggeration). At her death in 1931, several news accounts reported her birth year as early as 1817 (a 31-year exaggeration).

Was Granny Dollar's father part of the Band of Chief McIntosh Creeks?

Granny's father lived a traditionally western life and was no more than 1/2 Cherokee (or Creek) if he had any Indian heritage at all. Also known as Tustunnuggee Hutke, William McIntosh was one of the most prominent chiefs of the Creek Nation. He lived in Coweta, Georgia, where he died in 1825. The Callaway family had arrived in Gwinnett County, Georgia around 1830 from middle Georgia. In fact, John Callaway was living in Jasper County, Georgia, about 60 miles from Coweta, in 1825. So, the Callaway family is likely to have had more connection to the Creek people at Coweta than to the

Cherokee people of Gwinnett (and further north). But there is no certain connection between John or William Callaway and the Creek people or the band of Chief McIntosh.

Was Granny Dollar's grandfather John Grier Callahan?

Nancy Callaway's father was John Callaway. His middle name is unknown. However, family tradition reports that his middle initial was S, not G.

Was Granny Dollar's great-grandfather William?

Yes, Nancy Callaway's great-grandfather was William Callaway. William Callaway died in Wilkes County, Georgia, around 1816. His minor orphans then moved first to Putnam County, GA (1820), then to Jasper County, GA.

Did Granny Dollar's great-grandmother marry General Hugh Holland after William's death?

Unknown. There was a landowner named John Holland living in Putnam County, Georgia, in 1820. There was a large family of Hollands living in Jasper County, Georgia, throughout the time (1820-1830) that John Callaway and his brothers lived there. Still, there is no record of a marriage between a Callaway and a Holland. Archibald Holland, born in 1778, was living in Jasper County, Georgia in 1820. He had a brother named Hugh Holland, who was born in 1772 in South Carolina and who served in the revolutionary war. But it is not known if there is a connection between the Callaway family and this Hugh Holland. Also, there is no record of a General named

Hugh Holland.

Was Granny Dollar's father married to two wives simultaneously, Mary Sexton and Cassie, each with their own families?

Sort of. Nancy Callaway's father William had only one legal wife, Mary Sexton. Around 1866, William left his family (although he never divorced Mary) and moved to Union County, Georgia, where he lived with Catherine Brown. Although William and Catherine had many children, they never married. Mary Callaway and her family remained estranged from William from the late 1860s until his death 20 years later in Union County, Georgia.

Did Granny Dollar's father sire 26 children by his two wives, plus many illegitimate children as well?

Uncertain. Mary Sexton had 12 known children (possibly 13), and Catherine Brown had ten known children. Together, they had 22 surviving and possibly 23 total children or more.

Did Granny Dollar have a neighbor named Victor who had two wives named Hettie and Charlotte?

Unknown.

Did Granny Dollar fight with a girl named Mary Pucket when she was a little girl?

Probably. Mary Pucket was the daughter of Elisha Bird

Pucket and Lucy McMurray. Mary was born around 1847 in Rockbridge, Gwinnett County, Georgia. Her father passed away around April 1858, and her mother remarried James Sexton, a first cousin of Nancy's mother, Mary Sexton. Mary Pucket and Nancy were neighbors and step-cousins, so they probably fought occasionally.

Did Granny Dollar's father serve the US in the "Indian War"?

No, William Callaway was too young to have served in this war. Nelson Dollar's father, Nelson Dollar, Sr., served in the Indian wars. Also, Nancy's grandfather (William's father) likely served in these wars since he is listed as a veteran and pensioner on at least one US Census.

Did Granny Dollar and her family hide in a saltpeter cave near Buck's Pocket to avoid the forced removal of the Cherokee people from DeKalb County?

No. Granny Dollar's father, William A. Callaway, was only 13 years old and living in Gwinnett County, Georgia when the Cherokee people were forced to migrate westward.

Did Granny Dollar's father get into a dispute in Alabama around 1840 with a man named Jukes, who was sentenced to the penitentiary, and whose four sons were all hanged?

Unknown. There were no known men named Jukes living in either the DeKalb/Jackson County areas of Alabama or the

Gwinnett/Forsyth County areas of Georgia in the described time frame.

Did Granny Dollar's family move around 1840 to a small town about 30 miles from Marthasville?

No. Nancy and her father, mother, and all of her siblings were born in Georgia; all but her mother (and possibly her father) were born in Sugar Hill, Gwinnett County. Her mother was born in Jackson County, Georgia. Atlanta was only called Marthasville for about three years, around 1837-1840, eight to eleven years before Nancy was born.

Did Granny Dollar's mother give birth to three sets of triplets?

No. There is a possibility that Mary Sexton gave birth to a set of twins.

Did one of William's two wives die before Granny Dollar turned 21 years old (around 1845)?

No, Mary Sexton Callaway lived until 1901, dying in Liberty, Blount County, Alabama. Catherine Brown "Callaway" (although she was never married to William) married after William's death and lived until 1910, dying in Cherokee County, North Carolina.

Did Granny Dollar haul goods for a company known as Kyle Brothers Wholesalers? And, to a merchant named George Pass?

Unknown. In 1863 Nancy would have been 15 years old, so it is unlikely she owned her own delivery business. However, it is possible that Nancy recalled helping her father or some other relative with such deliveries. George B. Pass was a Merchant from White County, Tennessee, who was living in Hall County, Georgia, by 1850. He married Frances Louise Green in Gwinnett County, Georgia, around 1854. He is listed as a very close neighbor (4 dwellings away) of the William Callaway family in the 1860 US Census in Cains, Georgia. George Pass died in Lynchburg, Virginia, during the Civil War, in November 1863, just before the Battle of Fredericksburg. George Pass's widow moved to Blount County, Alabama, where many of the Callaways also moved. Also living nearby were brothers Thomas and Jasper Kyle. But these brothers were farmers rather than merchants.

Was Granny Dollar engaged to Tom Porter, the son of a merchant near Atlanta who died during the civil war?

Unknown, but unlikely. There was a Thomas R. Porter (b. abt 1840), the son of a farmer, living in nearby Cumming, Georgia, in 1860. Thomas R. Porter served in Company D of the 56th Georgia Infantry. He died at Enterprise Mississippi in August 1863. Another man, Thomas L. Porter, was the son of a hotel keeper in nearby Flowery Branch, Hall County, Georgia. He died shortly after the Civil war in May 1865. Both of these men were substantially older than Nancy Callaway, who was 13 at the beginning of the war.

Did Granny Dollar's father serve in the Civil War? Did he die at the battle of Atlanta?

Yes and no. William Callaway served for six months in the Georgia State Troops (Home Guard), serving most of his term in the Atlanta area. He survived the war.

Did Granny Dollar take in a woman named Madge Cole, along with her five children, and care for them for three years?

Unknown. This claim is likely a reference to a woman named Nettie Lavinia Dobbs Cole (also called Seletha Cole), a neighbor of the Callaway family in the Buford/Cains area in 1860. Levinia Cole was the wife of blacksmith Osborne Cicero Cole and the mother of six children. Osborne Cole died in May 1863 in Chancellorsville, Virginia. Netty Cole died in Gwinnett County in 1885 and is buried at Ebenezer Baptist Church Cemetery in Dacula. While it is possible that the Callaway family took Nettie Cole and her children in, it is more likely (though there is no evidence) that Nancy Callaway moved in with the Cole family to help them with their farming and household chores. In the 1880 Census, Nancy (age 32) is recorded living in her elderly grandparents' household. She likely moved there to assist them with their farm and household responsibilities.

Did Granny Dollar return to Alabama and marry Nelson Dollar "about 40 years after the Civil War ended" when she was 79 years old? Or did she marry "Wilson" Dollar when she was around 35 or 40 years old?

Nancy Callaway likely migrated to Alabama around 1893 and was already there when her grandmother's will was probated in 1900. She married Nelson Dollar in 1909 at the age of 61.

Were all of Granny Dollar's siblings dead before January 1928?

No. Nancy Callaway's full brother, James Noah Callaway, lived until 1952. Half-brother, John Joseph "Joe" Callaway, lived until 1955. At least 11 of her siblings and half-siblings were alive when Nancy made this claim to Sadie Shrader in 1927.

Did Granny Dollar have three half-brothers named Shadrach, Meshach, and Abednigo?

No. This is a fanciful "fact" that, no doubt, Nancy enjoyed telling people.

Did Granny Dollar have three sisters named Roxie Ann, Georgie Ann, and Texie Ann?

Almost. Nancy Callaway had a sister named Georgia Ann and a half-sister named Texanna (Texie Ann).

Was Granny Dollar distantly related, as some have claimed, to Griff Callahan, the son of a prominent citizen of DeKalb County, Alabama? Was she related to Theada Ovalee Wood, who married Cleo W. Chandler?

No, the Griff Callahan family of Jackson County, Alabama, is well-documented and is not related to the Callaways of Gwinnett and Wilkes Counties, Georgia.

Theada Ovalee Wood was the great granddaughter of Nelson Dollar, Jr.'s second cousin Martha Verlinda Dollar, who died at Grove Oak in Dekalb County in 1935. This makes her the third cousin (three times removed) of Granny Dollar's husband, Nelson Dollar, Jr.

Did Granny Dollar have any children?

Unknown. Records are inconsistent. Granny Dollar told journalist Winifred Black that she had children. In the 1910 US Census records, Nancy recorded that she had given birth to 2 children, neither of which survived.

What herbs did Granny Dollar use?

Granny claimed to use the following herbs:

- Ratsbane-*Chimaphila maculata*, or spotted wintergreen or rheumatism root
- Gentian root - *Gentiana lutea,* Great Yellow Gentian, for digestive problems, fever, hypertension, muscle spasms, parasitic worms, wounds, cancer, sinusitis, and malaria
- Rue -*Ruta graveolens*, herb of grace, used as an antidote to poisonous snake bites (of which Granny Dollar claimed three). Granny claimed it was used for "a brain that was pining"
- Crushed muscle or clamshells - acid indigestion, fatigue and to stop a hemorrhage

What happened to Milford Howard and Vivian Stella Howard?

After Granny died in 1931, Milford Howard rented her cabin to Forest and Edna Crow and their children. By 1937, Howard remodeled Granny Dollar's cabin and made it his home part of the year, living part-time in California. Howard divorced his second wife and cousin, Vivian, in 1936 after she moved to Florida and neglected to come home. Afterward, he turned his attention to one final project—building a memorial to his first wife. He spent the next year frantically constructing the Sallie Howard Memorial Chapel, dedicating it on June 27, 1937. Like everything he did, he started with high hopes. But, after a series of compromises and shortfalls, he was left completing the project mostly through his own labor and using inferior materials. Exhausted, he then returned to California, where he died on December 28th of the same year. The Chapel still stands today and is a frequented sightseeing destination in Mentone, AL. Stella Vivian Lloyd Harper Howard lived on, passing away on August 7, 1957, in San Benito, California, at the age of 78.

Who was Milford Howard's wife Sarah "Sallie" Lankford?

Milford first married Sarah Ann Lankford in December 1883. She was the daughter of Peter Green Lankford and Sarah Ann Hammock of Fort Payne, Alabama. On October 28, 1925, she died in Los Angeles, California, and was interred at Forest Lawn Memorial Park (Glendale, California).

Was Vivian Stella Lloyd related to Milford Howard?

According to Historian Elizabeth S. Howard, Vivian Stella

Lloyd was the daughter of Milford Howard's first cousin, Lula Ivey, making them first cousins once removed. Howard, however, claimed they were second cousins. My own research shows that they were not closely related.

What happened to Sadie Shrader and her husband Erskine?

Erskine and Sadie Shrader had six children. The eldest was Agnes Inez Shrader (b. 1915) who married William Daniel Butler. The second was Charles Theodore Shrader (b. 1917). The third was Dora Pauline Shrader (b. 1919), who married a Hawkins. The fourth was Willard Volstead Shrader (b. 1923). The fifth was Milford Shrader (b. 1926). The sixth was Herbert Clay Shrader (b. 1928).

George W. Erskine Shrader was convicted of incest in August 1934 and sentenced to serve from one to seven years in prison. He served exactly one year and was released on August 23, 1935. Sadie taught at Rock Bridge through 1935. According to the 1940 census, Sadie and Erskine divorced and, for the 1936 school year, Sadie moved to High Point, Alabama, on Sand Mountain and taught at Pea Ridge. She was on the school staff for the 1937 school year but did not end up working as she was stricken with cancer. Erskine Shrader moved to Fabius, Jackson County, Alabama. On December 18, 1937, 11-year-old Milford Shrader died in an accident (see below). Two months and two days later, on February 20, 1938, Sadie Shrader died of colon cancer. George W. Erskine Shrader lived until 1968, dying in the hospital at Summerville, Georgia.

What happened to Sadie and Erskine Shrader's son, Milford Shrader?

On Saturday morning, December 18, 1937, 11-year-old Milford Shrader was killed at the Palmer sawmill when his hand and a rubber coat he was wearing got caught and wound around a drive shaft, slinging him to death. He died en route to Summerville hospital shortly after the accident. On February 9, 1938, 11 days before his mother would pass away, Milford was awarded a posthumous 4H diploma.

Where did the chapter names come from?

The Chapter names are taken from quotes attributed to Granny Dollar.

What happened to Granny's neighbor and friend Clara Sharp Abbot?

After the murder of her husband, William Abbot, Clara moved to the valley near Battelle to live with her mother and stepfather. After the birth of her daughter Willa Mae, she married Frank Smith Thacker (who was 31 years older than her), at the age of 23 on Aug 7, 1924. Thacker was a native of Reeceville, Ohio. Before moving to Alabama, he worked for the Ringling Brothers Circus. He moved to the Fort Payne area around 1920. He was a teacher at DeKalb County High School and originated the first band there. He died in 1955 at the age of 85. Clara continued to live in Fort Payne for 17 more years, passing away on Oct 25, 1972, at the age of 71.

What happened to Granny's half-brother-in-law William Michael Waters?

William Michael Waters took a bus to Detroit, Michigan, to visit his sister Emily Waters Harmon - Mohan (age 72) for his 94th Birthday. There was some trouble upon boarding the bus because Michael wanted to take his rifle on the bus. He is said to have proclaimed, "I ain't goin' up 'round them damn Yankees without it!" After much debate, the bus driver allowed him to travel with his gun. According to some family members, Mike Waters passed away in 1971 at the age of 111.

What do Callaway family legends say about William A. Callaway?

It is no surprise that stories of William Callaway's life were not accurately told in the Callaway family. Granny Dollar said that her father was a 6'5" Indian who died in the Civil War. California Savannah Callaway told stories about her father too. In her version, William Callaway was a saddle maker that took off in a wagon for Tennessee to find work and "was never heard from again." Most of the family stories involve William and his father being owners of a large plantation with between 30 and 90 slaves.

Do we know any of the students, teachers, administrators, visitors, neighbors, etc., that may have known Granny Dollar at The Master School or River Park?

Students (Master School)

- Houston Craig of Broomtown
- Gunter Bailey of Bailey's Chapel
- Mary Sharp of Fort Payne
- Cora Sharp of Fort Payne
- Ethel Sharp of Fort Payne
- May Goss

Students (New Union Elementary, River Park, Alabama)

- Ruby Stallings
- Bill Blalock
- Andrew Wills
- Joe Howell
- Annie Bell Wisters
- Ethel Wills
- Eula Cardell
- Grace Crow

Workers

- Joe Biddle

Teachers (The Master School)

- Lucille Price
- Catherine A. McMenamin (of Chicago)
- Phillip Garfield McCurdy (Also taught/managed at Rock Bridge)

Visitors

- Willie and Ida Culpepper (w/ children, Rosie and D. L.) (The Culpepper children may have been students.)
- Miss Mintie Mason of Valley Head
- Miss Nellie Rogers
- Miss Jewell Bryant (teacher at nearby Rockbridge school)
- Frank and Stella Fischer (The Fischer children may have been students.)
- Sidney Hulgan
- Charley Baker (Also a New Oregon neighbor. He mined coal.)
- Winifred Black (Journalist from San Francisco)
- Henry B. Brock (Fort Payne Merchant)
- William V. Jacoway (Fort Payne, Postmaster)
- Mr. and Mrs. Dink Gilliam[184]
- Hardie and Stella Fischer
- Mr. and Mrs. Bob Little (and children)
- Irby Fischer
- Carrell Culpepper
- Jessie Frazier "Dee" Gilliam
- Mrs. Lela York
- Mr. and Mrs. T. N. Gray
- Floyd Cordell
- Frances Kirby (She sang at Granny's funeral)
- Alex Lankford (store owner)

Custodian (The Master School)

- Farmer Sharp

Administrators (The Master School)

- Stella Harper
- Milford Howard

Neighbors (1930)

- Knox and Kate McCurdy
- Charlie and Annie McCurdy
- Preston and Addie McCurdy
- John and Martha Burnett
- Martha Miller
- Samuel and Martha Keith
- James and Edna Marrow
- Harry and Bonny Shaffer
- Mack and Sadie McCurdy
- Erskine and Sadie Shrader
- Ida Reba Carr (teacher at New Union Elementary)
- Joseph Cordell
- Joe Cordell (son of Joseph)
- David Keith

What do we know about the practices of granny midwives in the late 1800s and early 1900s?

Among the herb cures described by "Aunt Granny" Lula Russeau (of Eufaula, Alabama, 1938) were:

The use of pine tops and mullein leaves for head colds; bitter weed for chills and fever;

Sage and catnip leaves, steeped for babies to cure hives;

Oil and turpentine, placed on the chest (heated) for colds.

Sassafras roots and asafoetida in a little sack on a green string, hung around the neck to ward off sickness.

Regarding midwifery, Aunt Granny said: "When I catch (deliver) a child and it's face up before it's born, it is a girl. If it is face down, it's a boy. I know that if I catch a girl with her face down, it is always bad luck. When a woman is threatened with a miscarriage, the best thing to give her is double tansy (a garden herb). Some grannies give dirt-dobber tea. When a woman starts the 'change,' rosemary tea is the best thing; you can usually find it in the cemetery." She claimed to have used black pepper tea and elbow tea (a little weed) but explained that she had no confidence in it. She said, "Yellow-root tea is good for morning sickness. Nightshade is another good herb for making salves for sore-head. When the afterbirth comes, burn it, then don't take up the ashes for four weeks, or it will mean bad luck. Then, wash all the clothes in the yard for good luck. If you put butterbean hulls in the road, it will keep your wife fertile. Don't give fish to a woman laying in bed, or it is sure death."

Aunt Granny described a process called quilling, in which the midwife would insert a hollow needle into a laboring woman's nose and blow red pepper deep into her nose. The resulting fits of coughing and sneezing would move hard labor on and lead quickly to a delivery. She has also placed a knife under a laboring woman's bed to 'cut' the labor pains.

Other common herbs and plant-based applications included hot ginger tea drunk before delivery to ease labor pains; catnip tea cured hives, "cleared up the liver", and insured a baby's first bowel movement; teas made of either chimney soot or apple tree and black gum bark stopped bleeding; pepper rattleweed, blueberry, raspberry, and bluebell, were all reputed to have hastened lengthy deliveries; "Angelico" or "Jellico" root helped alleviate afterbirth pains.

Aunt Granny also provided the following superstitious beliefs, which represent the types of readings and superstitions that Granny Dollar practiced: if you drop a knife or fork, somebody is coming [to visit]; if you want your wife to have children, throw cowpeas in the big road; if a screech owl screeches near the house, somebody in your family is going to die; when the frogs hollow, it's going to rain; if a black cat licks her fur the wrong way, it means a fight in the family; if a rooster crows in the first part of the night, hasty news; if you put your right shoe on first, or put a hat on the bed, that is bad luck; if you drop your dishrag, that means somebody far away is hungry; if your right eye itches, you are going to be in Georgia; if your left eye itches, you're going to get mad; if your right hand itches, you are going to get money or get a letter; if your foot itches, you are going to a 'strange land' (the cemetery is one of those 'strange lands'); if a rooster comes up on the porch and sticks his head in the door and crows, somebody is coming; if a rooster comes up in the house and sticks his head out of the door, somebody is going to die; if a cow lows at night, somebody is going to die; and if a snake comes in the house, that is the devil.

According to some sources, during labor, midwives generally made use of their knowledge of the birth process and the female anatomy as well as some simple equipment, medicinal herbs, and supernatural techniques to ensure successful delivery. Many midwives conducted intrauterine examinations during labor to ensure that the baby entered the birth canal in a proper "head first" position, and some adjusted a fetus that was entering improperly.

Dellie Lewis, who was born in slavery, recalled to writer Mary A. Poole, that her grandmother would make tea of spice and cloves with "a little whiskey" and gave it to a woman after childbirth to help her to expel the afterbirth. She also made a tea out of watermelon seed as a remedy for kidney stones.

What do we know about "conjuring" traditions in DeKalb County?

Classy Martin, who was formerly enslaved in DeKalb County, was interviewed by the Works Progress Administration in the late 1930s. Martin was born in Alabama around 1845. Martin recalled a woman treated by conjuring folk healers in DeKalb County when she was young. She recounted the woman, who had fallen ill after chewing on the bark of a tree. The woman was treated with boiled herbs and roots, and the conjurers offered "mumbling and hand waving." Martin recalled that "after she was conjured," flying insects crawled out of the pores of the woman's skin. Martin said, whenever someone died, they would put a cloth over each mirror to prevent evil spirits from taking the quicksilver. She advised, however, when her own mother became ill and lost a great deal of weight, she opted to go to a doctor in Birmingham and bought drugs from a normal drugstore to heal herself.

William W. Ellison compiled an interesting 'cure' for thrush in *Alabama Superstitions*: "Thrush, or sore mouth, need cause no alarm. Simply brew tea of nine saw bugs and have the child drink it. If this fails, it is best to send for a 'granny woman' who will cross two sticks in his mouth, utter some gibberish, and a cure will have been affected."

What happened to Winifred Black?

Winnifred Black died at her home on San Francisco's Marina after an illness of many weeks on May 25, 1936. Her funeral was a civic ceremony in San Francisco, with her body lying in state in the City Hall. She was buried at Holy Cross Cemetery in Colma, California.

Is the date on Granny Dollar's tombstone wrong?

The date on Granny Dollar's gravestone states that she died on January 25, 1931. But the Fort Payne Journal reported her death in their January 22, 1931 issue. A notice in the January 28, Journal, reported that she passed away "last Sunday night." Since January 25 was the "last" Sunday night, many researchers, including those who erected her tombstone in the 1970s, believed that she died on that day. But, since the article was a reproduction of a letter written by Milford Howard on

January 22nd, the paper was referring (unintentionally) to the Sunday night, one week earlier, January 18, 1931. According to Howard's letter, she died "at midnight." So, they deemed her to have died on January 19, 1931, and this date is consistent with her death certificate and six days before the date listed on her gravestone.

Is Granny Dollar related to the Callaways who founded Callaway Gardens?

Yes, Callaway Gardens, a 6,500-acre resort complex located in Pine Mountain, Georgia, just outside of LaGrange, draws over 750,000 visitors annually. It was founded in 1952 by Granny Dollar's fourth cousin, Cason Jewell Callaway.

Is Granny Dollar related to the Callaways who founded Callaway Golf and Callaway Apparel?

Yes, Callaway Golf was founded by Granny Dollar's fourth cousin (first cousin of Cason Jewell Callaway) and LaGrange, Georgia native Ely Callaway Jr. in 1982.

Are ghost stories still told about Granny Dollar?

In 2001, Randy Russell and Janet Barnett wrote *Ghost Dogs of the South*. That book tells the story of the ghosts of Granny Dollar and Looksee, her beloved Great Dane, who are said to still roam the foothills of the Appalachians. According to the authors, the ghosts are seen from time to time, usually in a swarm of bees. Such stories, like a game of telephone, continue to take on fresh forms as storytellers pass them on.

As late as 2016, visitors to the area have claimed to have seen the ghosts of Granny Dollar and Buster. The author has spent many nights camping in DeSoto Park and has never seen the ghost of either Granny Dollar or Buster.

Is Granny Dollar connected to the cave complex near Woodville, Jackson County, Alabama, known as "Callahan Cave?"

No. Callahan Cave was purchased from an unrelated woman (ironically) named Nancy Callahan in 2014. The cave was on property that the Callahan family had owned for decades. Before 2014, the cave was formally known as Stephens Gap Cave. The Stephens Gap Cave was not suitable for the mining of saltpeter. Another cave, Sauta Cave, which was nearby, was informally known as Callahan's Cave. But, Sauta cave was highly trafficked during the 1830s and could not have served as a hideout.

Do we know where Granny Dollar lived?

- Around 1900, Granny and Nelson Dollar were living near Dogtown in an area called Brandon
- By 1905, Nelson Dollar was homesteading 40 acres in the New Oregon/Fischer's Mill area
- By 1910, Granny and Nelson were living in Kensington, Walker County, Georgia
- By 1919, Granny and Nelson were living in the Crow Gap area north of Mentone near the present-day Ponderosa Girls Camp
- By 1923, Granny was living alone at River Park (present-

day DeSoto State Park)
- Granny also reported that she and Nelson Dollar had also lived near the brow on the "Oliver Place" near the Tutwiler House ("Idyllspot")

Pictures

Nancy Emeline Callaway Dollar

John Callaway (Granny's Grandfather)

William Anderson Callaway (Granny's Father)

Mary Garret Sexton (Granny's Mother)

The Callaway Family around 1855 (L-R William, Matilda, John A, Mary E, Mary Sexton, Sarah M, Nancy E

Granny Dollar's Cabin

The Ruins of Granny Dollar's Cabin

PICTURES

John Albert Callaway (Brother)

William Asbury Callaway (Brother)

Frances L Callaway (Sister)

Sarah Missouri Callaway (Sister)

DeSoto Falls

DeSoto Park Road ca 1936

PICTURES

Georgia Ann Callaway (Sister)

James Noah Callaway (Brother)

Milford W. Howard

Stella Vivian Harper Howard

Milford Howard's Cabin at River Park

The Ruins of the Master School

The Alpine Lodge

The Master School Under Construction 1923

Island Ford Baptist Church, Gwinnett County, Georgia

Callaway Cabin, Washington County, Georgia

Sarah Ellen McCurdy (Sadie Shrader) 1914

Sadie Shrader's Gravestone (New Home Baptist Church, Valley Head, Alabama)

Rockbridge School ca 1919

Index

A

Abbeville Herald, 106
Abbot, 101–3, 110, 125, 171, 172, Abbots, 101, 183
Albany, Georgia, 38
Albertville, Alabama, 23
Allatoona Lake, 87
Anderson, 73, 75, 99, 111, 113, 169, 178, Anderson's, 99
Apalachee River, 73
Appalachia, 7, 12, 35, 42;
Appomattox Courthouse, 66, 89
Athens, Georgia, 41
Atlanta, Georgia, 21, 47, 65, 75, 77, 90, 92, 95, 100, 118–20, 168, 174. 181, 182

B

Bailey, 127, 184; Bailey's Chapel, 127
Baker, 50, 54, 128, 175, 176
Bankhead, 39
Barnett, 134
Bartow County, Georgia, 87
Battelle, Alabama, 102, 125, 161, 184
Bearden, 98
Beauregard, 86
Beeson's Gap, 25

Bennett, 59
Berry, 8, 9
Biddle, 127
Birmingham, 11, 26, 98, 108, 133, 160-62, 164, 166, 167, 169-73, 176
Black, 30–32, 34, 38, 39, 44, 59, 63, 111, 122, 128, 130, 131, 133, 163, 171, 172; Black's, 31, 172
Blairsville, Georgia, 96
Blanche. 14
Blount County, Alabama, 78, 79, 81, 82, 118, 119, 177, 178, 181
Bonaparte, 40, 41
Brandon, Alabama, 135
Brogdon 179
Broomtown, Alabama, 82, 127
Brown, 54, 78, 83, 84, 88, 89, 116, 118, 177, 179
Brunswick, Georgia, 9, 163
Bryant, 128, 166
Buckner's Corps, 65
Buck's Pocket, 9, 10, 44–46, 113, 117, 163, 167, 174
Buford, Georgia, 75, 120, 179
Buncombe County, North Carolina, 78
Burnett, 129
Burton, 66, 177, 179
Buster, 3–5, 108, 109, 135, 161
Bynum, 59

C

Cains, Georgia, 119, 120
Callaway, 73–86, 88–97, 105, 111, 113–21, 126, 134, 177–82
Caldwell, 27, 28

Callahan, 19–21, 33, 46, 48, 84, 113–15, 121, 135, 166, 168, 172, 173, 175, 178, 180, 181

Callaway, 73–86, 88–97, 105, 111–20, 125, 133, 165–70

Campbell, 38

Canada, Union County, Georgia, 84; Canada Creek, 83; Canada District, 91; Canada Valley, 95

Canton, Georgia, 87, 88

Cardell, 127

Carr, 129

Cartersville Fault, 87

Cedartown, Georgia, 14

Celera, Alabama, 55

Centre, Alabama, 27, 174

Chancellorsville, Virginia, 120

Chandler, 121, 174

Charleston, South Carolina, 85

Chattahoochee River, 53, 75, 76

Chattanooga, Tennessee, 15, 24, 27, 81, 101, 170, 185

Chattanooga-Birmingham Highway, 27

Chattooga County, Georgia, 82

Chavies, Alabama, 25, 166

Cherokee County, Alabama, 78, 87, 88, 118, 174

Chester Mine, 88

Chicago, Illinois, 127

Chickamauga, Georgia, 65, 66

Clarke, 93

Clemens, 96

Cloudmont, Georgia, 27, 165

Coffeetown, Alabama, 19, 43–47, 167, 174

Cole, 21, 47, 120

Coley, 38

Colma, California, 133
Coosa District, 95; Coosa River, 27
Cordell, 82, 105, 128, 129, 164, 184
Coweta County, Georgia, 114, 172
Craig, 127
Cross, 81, 82
Crossville, Alabama, 23
Crow, 123, 127, 184
Crow Gap, 102, 135, 161, 165, 183
Culpepper, 128
Cumming, Georgia, 67, 75, 88, 119

D

Dacula, 120
Dade County, 39
Dahlonega, Georgia, 64, 90, 92, 96, 97, 181
Darlington, South Carolina, 57
Davis, 28, 91, Davis Gap, 25
Dawson County, 98–100, 103, 182
Dawsonville, Georgia, 103
Dekalb County, Alabama, 8, 13, 16–18, 22–24, 28, 33, 40, 41, 44, 45, 48, 53, 58–60, 62, 63, 67, 68, 81, 84, 100, 105, 117, 121, 122, 125, 132, 161, 162, 165–69, 174, 176, 185
DeSoto Caves, 26; DeSoto Falls, 16, 26, 28, 166, 170–72; DeSoto River, 26, 31; DeSoto State Park, 16, 26, 28, 31, 109, 135, 166, 170–72
Dixie Highway, 26
Dodd, 67, 179
Dogtown, Alabama, 135
Dollar, 4, 5, 10–14, 17–19, 21–23, 26, 28–32, 36, 38, 42–49, 52, 53, 54, 58, 59, 60–69, 73, 76, 77, 81, 82, 84, 86, 98, 101–123,

124, 125, 130, 132–35, 148–56, 170–80
  Donaldson, 88
  Driskill, 76, 180
  Dukes, 45

E
  Elbert County, 81
  Ellison, 133
  Emerson Fault, 87
  Etowah River, 51, 87
  Euchella Band of Cherokee, 51
  Eufaula, Alabama, 129, 165

F
  Fabius, Alabama, 124
  Finch, 58
  Fischer, 128, 166; Fischer's Mill, 63, 81, 135
  Flarity, 101
  Flowery Branch, Georgia, 120
  Floyd County, Georgia, 51, 101
  Forsyth County, Georgia, 44, 46, 53, 62, 64, 67, 68, 75, 77, 114, 118, 172, 176
  Fort Payne, Alabama, 8, 10–12, 14, 17, 18, 22, 23, 25, 28, 30, 34, 41, 42, 48, 68, 103, 105, 106, 109, 123, 125–28, 133, 163, 165–68, 170, 184
  Fort Sumter, South Carolina, 85
  Foster, 59
  Franklin County, Georgia, 73
  Fredericksburg, Virginia, 119

G

Gadsden, Alabama, 15, 24, 59, 152
Gaiman, 1
Gamblin, 84
Gibson, 55
Gilliam, 104, 105, 128, 184
Gilmer County, Georgia, 51, 99, 183
Glendale, California, 123
Gravitt 161
Gray, 128, 175
Greene 176
Griswell, 91
Guinness World Records, 55
Guion-Miller Roll, 52
Guntersville, 168, 174
Gurley, 93, 94, 171
Gwinnett County, Georgia, 53, 64–66, 73–78, 80–82, 89, 90, 114, 117–21, 172, 176, 177, 179082

H

Habersham County, Georgia, 100
Hall County, Georgia, 67, 73, 76, 119
Hall's Store, 27
Hamilton County, Tennessee, 81, 83
Hammock, 123
Hammondville, Alabama, 167
Harbison, 91
Hardin County, Tennessee, 86
Harper, 9, 123, 129, 163
Hawkins, 124
Hearst, 30
Higgens, 81

Holland, 33, 46, 115, 178, 179
Hollywood, California, 9
Howard, 4–6, 8–16, 22, 26, 30–34, 36, 44–48, 63, 68, 104–7, 111, 114, 122-24, 129, 133, 134, 161-68, 170-74
Howell, 127
Hudspeth, 98, 99
Hulgan, 128
Huntsville, Alabama, 25, 108
Hutke, 114, 172

I

Ingenthron, 39, 173
Isbill 163
Ivey, 124

J

Jackson, 18, 45, 46, 73, 76, 78, 100, 103, 117, 118, 121, 124, 135, 166–68, 173, 182
Jacoway, 127
Jasper County, Georgia, 74, 75, 114, 115, 178, 179
Johnson, 39, 63, 81, 173, 176, 177, 179, 182
Johnston, 86
Jones, 67
Jude, Alabama, 18, 167
Jukes, 20, 33, 45, 47, 117

K

Keith, 56, 57, 105, 129, 184
Kensington, Georgia, 63, 135
Kerby, 184, Kirby, 128
Knoxville, Tennessee, 65

INDEX

Kuykendall, 44, 45, 161, 174
Kyle, 21, 47, 118, 119, 174

L

Lafayette, Georgia, 65
Lafferty 173
Lafon, 82
LaGrange, Georgia, 134
Lahoosage, Alabama, 26
Lankford, 122, 128
Lathemtown, Georgia, 88
LaTourrette, 174
Lawrenceville, Georgia, 65, 75
Lebanon, Alabama, 18, 95, 96
Lewis, 56, 57, 132
Liberty, Alabama, 78, 82, 118
Lloyd, 9, 123, 124
Lookout Creek, 23
Lookout Mountain, 5, 6, 8–10, 13, 15–18, 21, 23–27, 29, 39, 61–63, 98, 101, 106, 107, 111, 162-65, 170, 172, 183, 184
Lowman, 98–101, 102, 103, 111, 182, 183
Lumpkin County, Georgia, 51, 83, 94, 168
Lunsford, 93, 176, 181
Lynchburg, Virginia, 119

M

Macedonia, Alabama, 39
Mahan School, 18
Marthasville (Atlanta), Georgia, 20, 47, 118, 168
Martin, 74, 75, 98, 101, 131, 167, 168
Mahan 18

Marietta 174
Martin 74, 75, 98, 101, 132, 179, 180
Mason, 128
Mays Gulf, 27
McCarter, 74
McCurdy, 17, 18, 127, 129, 166, 167
McIntosh, 33, 46, 113, 114, 172
McMenamin, 127
McMurray, 117
Mentone, Alabama, 3, 13, 21, 25–28, 30, 39, 43, 63, 101, 111, 123, 135, 160, 161, 163, 170, 171, 173, 183, 184
Meriwether County, Georgia, 75
Miller, 129
Mohan, 126
Montgomery, West Virginia, 56
Montgomery Advertiser, 57, 165, 174
Montgomery Alabama, 56
Moorman, 26
Mullins, 88

N

Nashville, Tennessee, 56
Nimblewill, 83, 94, 97, 103

O

Oconaluftee Band (Cherokee), 51
Orange, Georgia, 88
Ozark Mountains, 39, 161, 173

P

Palmer, 83, 125

Panama City, Florida, 58
Pass, 26, 47, 86, 118, 119, 125, 134
Peek, 53
Phillips, 39, 98, 101, 165, 183
Pintlala Creek, 56
Pisgah, Alabama, 18, 100
Pittsburg Landing, Tennessee, 86
Powell's Store, 27
Preston's Division, 65
Pucket, 33, 116, 117
Putnam County, Georgia, 74, 115, 178

Q

Qualla Tribal Land, 52

R

Ragen, 77, 80
Randolph County, Arkansas, 14
Rayle, Georgia, 74
Reese, 17
Ripley's Believe it or Not, 58
Rockbridge, 116, 128
Rome, Georgia, 13, 14, 51
Rosalie, Alabama, 18
Russeau, 129, 165
Russell, 134

S

Saltville, Virginia, 65
Sand Mountain, Alabama, 9, 18, 19, 23–25, 39, 58, 124, 163, 166, 167, 172, 174

Sardis 167
Satterfield, 96, 97
Sauty, 44, 174; Sauta Cave, 44, 135, 168, 174
Savannah, Georgia, 50, 63–65, 81, 126, 177
Scottsboro, Alabama, 25, 103, 166
Seabolt, 83, 93, 96, 181, 182
Sexton, 19, 46, 73, 76, 78, 80, 82, 113, 116–18, 179
Shaffer, 129
Sharon, Pennsylvania, 98
Shiloh Church, 86
Shrader, 17–19, 22, 30, 32-34, 44–47, 63, 112, 122, 124, 125, 129, 166–69, 172
Smith, 39, 57, 58, 75, 100, 101, 125, 163, 139, 170
St. Elmo, Tennessee, 25, 81
Strayhorn, 43, 173
Suches, Georgia, 83, 91, 93
Sugar Hill, Georgia, 67, 73–75, 77, 87, 88, 118, 177
Suwanee, Georgia, 75
Sylvania, Alabama, 18

T

Taney County, Missouri, 39
Teloga, Georgia, 81
Thacker, 125
Tocoa, Georgia, 51
Trenton, Georgia, 23, 24
Tutwiler, 13, 26, 136, 165, 169

V

Valley Head, Alabama, 18, 23, 26, 101, 128, 165, 169, 175, 183

W

Wade Gap, 11, 26, 165
Waleska, Georgia, 87
Walker County, Georgia, 13, 39, 63, 101, 135, 184
Walker's Chapel, 27
Walnut Fork, 76
Walton County, Georgia, 73
Washington, DC, 14, 15, 57, 74, 169, 182
Wehunt, 83, 94
Wilkes County, Georgia, 74, 115, 121, 178, 179
Willet, 107, 110
Williams, 57, 93, 165, 166, 171, 181, 182
Willingham, 41
Wills Creek, 23; Wills Valley, 23–25, 102, 169
Windham, 108, 109
Wisters, 127
Woodville, Alabama, 135, 168

Y

York, 128, 174, 183

Notes

INTRODUCTION

1. Masters, Harriet P., *"A Study of the Southern Appalachian granny woman Related to Childbirth Prevention Measures."* (2005). Electronic Theses and Dissertations. Paper 1004. https://dc. Etsu. Edu/etd/1004 - "The specifics of folk medicine practices detailed in the Haun text *The Hawk's Done Gone and Other Stories,* support the idea that granny women received specific herbal remedies through oral tradition, and that a midwife in training received information through an apprenticeship with an elder midwife."

2. According to *The Birmingham News* (Birmingham, Alabama) 22 Jan 1931, Page 1, Granny Dollar was "widely known" as a midwife, folk healer, and fortune teller among the hundreds of residents of the Mentone area and the thousands of summer tourists that visited that area. However, it is among the journalists and historians that her identity as a granny woman has been lost.

3. Masters, Harriet P., *"A Study of the Southern Appalachian granny woman Related to Childbirth Prevention Measures."* (2005). Electronic Theses and Dissertations. Paper 1004. https://dc. Etsu. Edu/etd/1004 Between 1900 and 1930, pregnancy was the second-largest killer of women of childbearing age in the United States. Also, 50% of all births were attended by midwives.

   In a spirit rooted in devotion, the women who fulfilled the role of granny woman aided and assisted those living around them, a role arising out of compassion and not on the foundation of financial gain, as would later be the case regarding the educated males who developed and implemented a campaign to eliminate the granny woman.

4. Ghost story - *Haunted Southern Nights, Volume 3, History and Haunting of the Mentone Area* By Deborah Collard · 2009

5. Wooten, Neal, *Granny Dollar,* Mirror Publishing, 2017

6. McPherson, Eddie, *Granny Dollar and the Trail of Tears,* 2018

NOTES

7 Lafferty, Sandra, *Behind the Scenes with Sandra Lafferty, 2017*
8 During the 1930s in the United States, the Works Progress Administration (WPA) developed the Federal Writers' Project to support writers and artists while attempting to document the country's shared history and culture. Among the pamphlets published by the WPA was one documenting a motor tour of the Mentone, Alabama area. Among the highlights of the tour is "the Granny Dollar Cabin." (Federal Writers Project, The WPA Guide to Alabama: The Camellia State, 2013 - originally published in 1941)
9 Gravitt, Margie, Kuykendall, James R., Howard, Mrs. Max J (Editor), *Famous DeKalb Indian, The DeKalb Legend,* Landmarks of DeKalb County, Inc., May 1972
10 The term "conjure" refers to Appalachian (and Ozark) folk magic practices. Other terms are "backwoods witchcraft," "granny magic," and "folk magic."
11 Mirror Publishing (June 4, 2017)

"I'M ALL ALONE WITH NO ONE TO LOVE ME"

12 In September 1928, Milford Howard, in his column for *The Birmingham News*, recalled "It was just after the opening of the Master School, almost 5 years ago, that Granny walked several miles to make our acquaintance." The Master School opened on Monday, September 3, 1923. So, it is reasonable to presume that she arrived at the school around October 1923.

Floyd Abbot advised that he and his mother Clara visited Granny Dollar and Nelson at their cabin above Battelle, Alabama, north of Crow Gap, sometime in the early 1920s and that Nelson Dollar passed away not long afterward. So, it can be reasonably presumed that Granny Dollar was living north of Crow Gap, and Mentone, immediately before coming to the Master School—a walk of about 10 miles. The site of the Dollar cabin north of Crow Gap is near present-day Ponderosa Bible Camp.

13 "Mother Hubbard" dresses were introduced to Vanuatu in the 1800s by Presbyterian missionaries in a bid to "cover" the local women.
14 *The Birmingham News* (Birmingham, Alabama) 22 Jan 1931, Page 1, "It may have been this sense of guardianship that made Buster a mean, vicious beast to everyone except 'Granny.' He was cordially hated by all

the men and women in the community, and feared by the children."

15 DeKalb County historically maintained a 'poorhouse'. The County Treasurer maintained an account to care for the poor, and County Commissioners appointed an individual to look after those maintained on a "poor list." For example, in 1894, William M. Barksdale was the county's "keeper of the poor." In July 1895, the county books indicate that $417.70 was expended to care for paupers in the first half of that year. In February 1896, Barksdale reported that six people were living in the poorhouse. In the 1920s in DeKalb County, there were many poor, but few who had no means to care for themselves. So, even the very poor feared the stigma of the label, "pauper."

16 When she first arrived at the school in the fall of 1923, Granny Dollar claimed to be "almost 100 years old." Milford Howard, in July 1927, reported her age as 101, meaning that he would have expected her to be 97 when she first arrived. While Howard reported her age as 101 in 1927, he also simultaneously estimated her age to be 106 or more, based on her "memory" of historical events.

17 As early as 1938, writers for the Federal Writers' Project had documented that Granny Dollar had been feared, in her lifetime, as a witch, and she had been known to threaten people with spells. While adults of Lookout Mountain viewed Granny mostly as a folk healer and fortune-teller, the children viewed her as a witch and feared her.

18 Nancy Dollar is documented in the 1900 US Census under the name "Emeline J. Dollar." In the 1920 US Census, she is documented as "Emley Dollar." In the 1930 US Census, she is documented as "Nancy M. Dollar." However, this is probably a misunderstanding by the Census taker, and should have been recorded as "Nancy 'Em' Dollar." She was known to have been called by many names, including Nancy, Emeline, Emily, Em, Granny, Grandma, and Lucy.

19 In *The Birmingham News* (Birmingham, Alabama) 12 Aug 1928, Page 50, Katherine H. Chapman reported that, when Granny Dollar was not smoking her almost ubiquitous pipe, she was using a snuff stick. A snuff stick is a small brush or stick used to deliver snuff to the gums. On many occasions, Granny was seen to be working, barefoot, in her garden with a snuff stick miraculously dangling from her lips.

20 In *The Birmingham News* (Birmingham, Alabama) 03 Jun 1928, Page 14, Milford Howard wrote that Granny Dollar had a "massive frame," and a

"voice like a foghorn." However, Winifred Black reported that Granny Dollar was "little and wiry."

21 Granny was known to make direct requests of people and to make fanciful threats if they did not comply. Many people were intimidated by her manner, but to others, she was considered harmless and endearing.
22 Granny was known to practice weather magic or weather divination.
23 Milford Howard wrote that it was good to hear Granny laugh as she told hair-raising stories to spellbound visitors.

"...A BRAIN THAT'S A PININ'"

24 The Master School was incorporated in Alabama in 1923. The trustees were M. W. Howard, Los Angeles, California; Stella Vivian Harper, Brunswick, Georgia; Claude Howard, Camden, Alabama; John B. Isbill, Fort Payne, Alabama; and Mamie B. Hansen, Los Angeles, California.
25 Smith, George. *Mountain Thinker and Experimenter*. Mentone, Alabama, 1939. Manuscript/Mixed Material. https://www. Loc. Gov/item/w-palh000024/
26 Howard, M. W., *Peggy Ware*. Los Angeles; J. F. Rowny Press, 1921
27 Howard said that after rushing to Buck's Pocket, he and Vivian both felt intuitively that it was not the right place to build The Master School. At this time, the southern end of Sand Mountain was more developed for farming, and therefore the land on that mountain was much more valuable than the land on nearby Lookout Mountain. Even in the bottom of Buck's Pocket, land, if it was available, was in smaller plots (40-80 acres). On Lookout Mountain, however, there were vast areas of untouched wilderness, and crop farming was less common. As a result, land was more affordable. Howard's intuition was right in that he knew that he could never afford to build his school at Buck's Pocket.
28 Howard would later add 250 acres to this site.
29 It is likely that the school was a part of a larger real estate investment scheme by Howard. His wife was successfully investing in development in California and, on Lookout Mountain, there were numerous efforts to develop tourist and summer home properties. Howard had purchased much more land (up to 1,000) acres adjacent to the school.
30 Substantial efforts were made to raise funds to support The Master School and the community did largely respond. As an example, In June 1924, a ladies club in Gadsden, Alabama held a luncheon to raise funds for

the school. The event was attended by more than thirty people and was quite successful. Also, Howard was fairly successful at soliciting broader interest in the school, and he and his cousin began, in 1925, to travel throughout the region engaging in public speaking events to solicit funds. According to the WPA, The Master School was discontinued when the state began to build schools to serve the remote mountain communities.

31 In 1925, the school became a summer camp for boys. Ownership was transferred to the Benevolent Order of National Defenders in 1926, and the campus was converted into a home and school for the widows and orphans of the order.

32 Farmer Sharp, whose three girls attended the Master School was serving as a handyman as early as the fall of 1923. Also, there were ongoing efforts to clear land, build additional buildings, and clear a road up Cordell Gap to support easier mail delivery to the school.

33 Howard receives much credit for the Granny Dollar phenomena. But, from the beginning, he had no intention of exploiting her story or even publicizing it. He even failed to comprehend that her presence as a mascot at the school might help him elicit sympathy and, therefore, contributions. He really viewed her presence as something of a nuisance. He was also greatly intimidated by Granny. She was a demanding tenant, and Howard had difficulty saying no to her. For example, when he first granted Granny permission to stay at his cabin, rather than "go to the poorhouse" as she feared, she immediately demanded a deed to the cabin. So, Howard simply decided to keep his distance.

34 Later writers would speculate that Granny Dollar simply began to walk through the Lookout Mountain countryside until she randomly happened upon the empty cabin of Howard's. This scenario, of course, is highly unlikely.

35 One Lookout Mountain writer wrote: "These folks who talk so much about 'helping the mountain people,' many of them don't stop to think how maybe we don't look with favor on the same things. The very things they value the highest may rate pretty low with us and 'vicey-vercy' as we used to say in the old *Bluebacked Speller*."

36 These activities are precisely the types of activities (along with fortune-telling) that Granny Dollar was known for participating in.

37 In The Birmingham News (Birmingham, Alabama), 28 May 1929, Page 4 story, Mrs. W. L. Murdock reported a visit to Granny Dollar's Cabin.

She stated that Granny, "hears all the gossip."

38 Howard specifically wrote that he and Granny were not previously acquainted.

39 Howard had moved back to California in 1919.

40 Granny, in interviews, said that she previously lived in what is known locally as the Oliver Place, and at the Leonard Reece Place, near Cloudmont next to the Tutwiler Place. She had most recently lived in the Phillips area at Crow Gap north of Mentone.

Loenard Harrison Reece was a lumberman from Valley Head. He lived on the brow of Lookout Mountain overlooking Big Will's Valley between Tutwiler Gap and Wade's Gap. He married Elizabeth Leah Shigley. The Reece family later relocated to Spartanburg County, South Carolina.

41 Couric, Gertha (interviewer): *Mid-Wives are Called Grannies*, in the Federal Writers' Project papers #3709, Southern Historical Collection, The Wilson Library, University of North Carolina at Chapel Hill, 1938

Lula Russeau, a former slave, was interviewed by Gertha Couric in Eufaula, Alabama in 1938. Interestingly, "Aunt Granny," as Russeau was known, also claimed to be an Indian.

The August 13, 1998 edition of *The Montgomery Advertiser* contained an article about Fort Payne and Mentone by Kathie Farnell. In that article, Farnell speculated that Granny Dollar earned her nickname, "Granny", from taking care of orphans and her own siblings after the Civil War. This demonstrates the press's misunderstanding of the tradition of the granny-midwife and failure to connect Granny Dollar to that tradition.

42 The origins of the title of Colonel can be traced back to colonial and antebellum times when men of the landed gentry were given the title "Colonel" to commission companies or for financing the local militias without actual expectations of command. It was common in the state of Georgia for lawyers admitted to the Bar to request, and be granted, the honorary title by the Governor.

"I REMEMBER MIGHTY WELL"

43 *The Progressive Farmer* often maintained a local reporter in DeKalb County. For example, in June 1828, Mr. and Mrs. F. D. Williams arrived in DeKalb and stayed for the summer with Miss Daisey Slone, with Mr.

Williams being there to represent the interests of *The Progressive Farmer*. So, it is possible that Sadie Shrader worked with a local representative of the Birmingham-based magazine to develop the Granny Dollar story.

44   It is not known why Nancy Dollar consistently used the false name, Callahan. It is possible that she used Callahan in 1909, when she married Nelson Dollar, to avoid a charge of bigamy (assuming she was previously married), and continued to use it thereafter. Prior to 1909, and as early as 1900, she was using the name Nancy (or Emeline) Dollar. Prior to that, in the early 1890's she was using her birth name.

45   New Oregon is also often referred to as Fischer Community.

46   Rock Bridge School was located near the north entrance of DeSoto Park at the present-day site of Rock Bridge Holiness Church. The school was open as early as the 1890s. It was closed at least once in the early 1900s and reopened in 1904. It was consolidated with Fischer School (New Oregon School) around 1936. Teachers at Rock Bridge included: Sarah Rains (the 1890s), Edna Allen (1904), Bulah Rice (1907), James A. Stephens (1911-1912), Edgar Tatum (1912-1913),Albert Howard (1914), Fred Igou (1915), Mary E. Thornberry (before 1920), Vonnie Lee Yarborough(1921-22), Jewel Bryant (1923), Mary Cunningham (1924), Garfield McCurdy (1926), Sadie Shrader (1927), and Hilda Fears (?-1936).

47   It is not clear where Erskine Shrader was working in 1927. Newspapers refer to his work at "Cloudland." This could possibly be one of the numerous camps in the area of New Oregon, or it could refer to the "Cloudland Hotel," a large 50-room resort hotel that was completed near Cloudland, GA in 1926.

48   The article was divided into two articles with the second appearing exactly one month later.

49   Sara Ellen McCurdy's great-great-grandfather, Elijah McCurdy, patented 160 acres in DeKalb County at Pine Ridge in May 1845. But, the McCurdy's had arrived in Alabama somewhat earlier, in 1837, when her great-grandfather patented 40 acres in Jackson County, Alabama near Scottsboro.

50   Before Sadie re-entered school to complete her degree, she had already obtained many years of experience operating (and teaching in) her own private school on Sand Mountain.

51   McCurdy attended "Normal School" at Chavies, receiving teacher training, prior to completing her high-school education at Fort Payne.

NOTES

52   Jude was located on Sand Mountain near the brow overlooking Wills Valley between Hamondville and modern-day Henegar, Alabama.

53   *The Fort Payne Journal* (Fort Payne, Alabama) 09 Dec 1925. By January 1926, *The Fort Payne Journal* reported that Garfield McCurdy had moved to Rock Bridge Elementary School.

54   Granny Dollar claimed to practice Cherokee "conjuring."

55   Shrader's article appeared in print in January 1928, so it is evident that her interview with Granny was done a bit earlier. During the interview, Granny mentioned that she had been widowed "four years ago." Since Nelson Dollar died in the spring of 1923, it is likely that the Shrader interview with Granny Dollar occurred sometime between the spring and fall of 1927. However, Sadie Shrader, in her article included a photo of Granny Dollar, which was taken on "the day of her 101st birthday." Milford Howard, in his column for *The Birmingham News*, reported on July 1, 1928, that Granny would turn 101 "this month." That means that the Sadie Shrader interview almost certainly occurred on the occasion of that birthday celebration in July 1928.

56   This would place Granny's purported birth year as 1826.

57   Coffeetown was the original name of modern-day Langston, Alabama in Paint Rock Valley in Jackson County, Alabama. Prior to the arrival of white settlers, the Creeks and Cherokees controlled the area that encompassed Coffeetown. In 1810, white settlers established a small township, named after the Coffee brothers, there. The town's first post office was established in 1845, and its first postmaster was Langston Coffee.

In July 1861, when Nancy was 13 years old, her father William patented 80 acres on Sand Mountain spanning the DeKalb and Jackson County boundary near the community of Kirby's Creek at the location of present-day Old Sardis Church. It is not clear that William ever occupied or improved this property, however, the property aligns closely with Nancy's description of being born "eight miles east of Coffeetown."

58   Milford Howard reported that William's second family was in North Carolina. Reporting the location as South Carolina is likely a mistake on Shrader's part.

59   There are two well-known saltpeter caves located in the area of Buck's Pocket. The first one, in Jackson County across the Tennessee River

near Guntersville, is Sauta Cave. A second, near Fort Payne, Alabama is Manitou Cave. Both were extensively mined for saltpeter before, and during, the Civil War period.

There is a cave near Woodville, Jackson County, Alabama called "Callahan Cave." However, there is no tradition of saltpeter being mined from this cave. It was named after a woman named (ironically) Nancy Callahan who owned the land where it is found until 2014.

60 Marthasville was the name briefly given to the town that would become Atlanta, Georgia. It was founded as a rail terminal in 1837 and first called Thrasherville (1839), then Terminus (1840). In 1842, locals changed the name to Marthasville, to honor the daughter of Governor Lumpkin. In 1845, the town was renamed to Atlantica-Pacifica (quickly shortened to Atlanta). So, the designation of Marthasville was only used for around three years and was only one of a series of names used for the tiny settlement and terminal station. Research shows that Atlanta was not known by Marthasville within Nancy Dollar's lifetime and the use of the name is inconsistent with the timeline given to Sadie Shrader.

61 Appalachian midwives, during this time, normally charged between $3 and $5 to attend a birth. Because midwives' patients could not often afford to pay them, these women frequently accepted food, goods, gifts, and favors in lieu of cash (Source: Scott, Shaunna, *Grannies, Mothers and Babies: An Examination of Traditional Southern Appalachian Midwifery*, University of California, Berkley)

62 Granny used a knife to trace out the lines in the palm of a visitor's hand in order to tell their fortune.

63 The Master School was not Milford Howard's first attempt to form a school. In October, 1917, Howard petitioned DeKalb County for a new school district and district 104 was formed. Howard built the Howard School on Kershaw Road, north of Fort Payne. This school operated successfully until the 1930s, when it was consolidated with the Fort Payne Schools.

64 As a contrast, it is noted that the March 11, 1853 issue of the Fort Payne Journal included an article entitled *DeKalb Women in Progressive Farmer*, which pointed out that three DeKalb County women were "spotted" in the March issue of *The Progressive Farmer*, "the South's leading magazine." While, in 1928, the local paper didn't seem to notice that a local woman had an article published in the same magazine. After the article was

published, the next mention of Sadie Shrader in the local paper was an October mention to indicate that she earned $455 per year as a teacher and a mention one week later that she and her husband had welcomed a baby boy.

"...WE ALL LIVED HAPPY TOGETHER."

65 The Cumberland Plateau is the southwestern part of the Appalachian Mountains. It includes much of eastern Kentucky and Tennessee, and portions of northern Alabama and northwest Georgia. In those states, it is the dissected plateau lands lying west of the main Appalachian Mountains.

66 Wills Valley is actually made up of two smaller valleys separated by ridges. One, called Big Wills Valley is separated from the other, Little Wills Valley by East Red Mountain or "Big Ridge." Several smaller valleys or coves extend from Big Wills Valley. These include Sand Valley and Ripshin, which are separated from Big Wills Valley by Shinbone Ridge.

67 Idyllspot was the summer home of Edward McGruder and Mary Anderson Tutwiler. It overlooked their 1,600-acre sportsmen's estate called "Winston Place" in Valley Head. He died by self-inflicted gunshot in September, 1932.

68 Colonel Walter Sumpter Smith (1897-1943) was an engineer, Army pilot, government aviation official, and promoter of aviation. He served as an Army pilot and instructor in World War I and afterwards as commandant of Roberts Field in Birmingham, AL, and helped to establish new air mail routes in the South during the late 1920s. In 1935 he was made head of the Airport Division of the Works Project Administration and was later appointed chairman of the Safety Board of the Civil Aeronautics Authority. In January 1939, he was appointed as chairman of the commission to build Washington National Airport. During World War II, he returned to active duty and was made chief of Transport and Facilities Division of Army Air Support in March 1942. On 24 January 1943 his aircraft disappeared over the Caribbean Sea. In 1943 he was posthumously awarded the Distinguished Service Medal.

69 In January 1924, in Alabama, 171 stills (and 12 automobiles) were seized by state law enforcement officers. Of the 200 felony arrests for various offenses, 129 were associated with illegal distilling. In March 1924, 31 cases were settled in DeKalb County courts. Of these, six were for distilling, three were for selling liquor, and eight were for public

drunkenness. Of the remaining 14 cases, at least some were for violations of parole associated with distilling.

70   Writer George Smith of Mentone wrote in the 1930s of life on Lookout Mountain. Smith recalled the many mills on the mountain and wrote that the grist mills ground grain "on shares." In other words, they accepted a share of the mill in return for the labor of grinding it for the farmers. The sawmills operated similarly offering to saw raw logs (delivered to the mill) into lumber for a 50% share of the sales proceeds. Otherwise, they charged $4.00 per thousand board feet for sawing.

71   Advertisements during this time claimed that summer temperatures at Mentone were as much as 10 degrees lower than in the valley.

72   Although most residents appreciated the injection of cash from the summer tourists, their opinions of them personally was mixed. One Mentone writer wrote, "Those foreigners who ride through the mountains in their fine cars, with their drivers dressed up like a policeman, or an army captain, call themselves 'tourists', call the mountains 'grand' and 'gorgeous.' But to us they mean a lot more than that. They're a living part of us."

73   In October 1923, around the same time that Granny Dollar first arrived at The Master School, Roy Workman submitted a note that was published in the *Chattanooga News*. He said that he had been engaged to chauffeur a party of tourists from a hotel in Mentone to DeSoto Falls during the summer. He took them the four miles in an old Ford and waited while they ate lunch and went swimming at the falls. When he returned them to their hotel in Mentone, he was shocked to be paid $3 for a few hours' work. He stated that it was the most money he had ever earned for a single day's work.

74   *The Birmingham News* (Birmingham, Alabama) 22 Jan 1931. Reporting that "Granny Dollar told fortunes for 'many hundreds' of tourists."

75   In March 1923, the *Fort Payne Journal* jokingly commented that "Will Autry has moved back to Lookout Mountain. Done got rich in the valley."

"I KEEP RIGHT ON WITH MY CONJURE"

76   Milford Howard wrote that he had 'mentioned' Granny Dollar occasionally, but had never written about her. Although she had lived prominently in the cabin on the Howard property for almost 4 and a half years, there is no indication that either Howard, or any other professional local

journalists, had taken much interest in Granny by this time. Howard had mentioned Granny Dollar in his *Birmingham News* column, on June 3, barely two months earlier, but he did not include many of her claims—only that she was 100 years old and an 'Indian.' He also wrote, "Granny has an imagination, I must confess." Howard also mentioned Granny on July 1 and July 22 in connection with a visit to the Alpine Lodge of Winifred Black. Again, he provides scarce details. On July 22, he reported that he had received details of a sketch written by Black about Granny.

In the August 12, 1928 issue of *the Birmingham News*, Journalist Dolly Dalrymple wrote a full-page column (*Alabama's Hills and Rills*) about a visit to DeSoto Falls, and Mentone. In the article, she mentions a visit to Milford Howard's Alpine Lodge and a previous visit to the lodge by journalist Winifred Black, but the article makes no mention of Granny Dollar. It is evident that her stories were mostly seen as tall tales, at least by professional journalists, and little effort was made to either report or verify them.

77   Winifred (*nee* Sweet) Black Bonfils

78   When The Master School closed, Howard built on to one of the dormitories to create "The Alpine Lodge," a large, sprawling estate intended as a summer resort. It had 3,500 square feet of balconies and porches and could accommodate 50 guests. The Lodge was designed by noted Auburn architect Gurley Bergin, who was asked to design the Lodge for free by Howard and his wife, who could not afford to pay an architect. Bergin agreed to the work after visiting River Park and meeting Granny Dollar. (Source: Volume LII, issue 14, November 8, 1928 issue of *The Plainsman*, the student newspaper of the Alabama Polytechnic Institute, now known as Auburn University)

The Lodge was completed in the summer of 1928 on the River Park estate. Howard envisioned the lodge as a place for artists to come for inspiration and to free themselves of disruptions. In April 1929, Howard sold the Alpine Lodge and much of his river park property to investors James G. B. Fletcher and W. W. Williams who operated it as the River Park Boys Camp. Fletcher and Williams also acquired rights to develop River Park, including more than 20 stone buildings and the "grandmother cabin," although Granny was still living there.

79   '*My Country Tis of Thee*' was a series of Sunday magazine articles written

by Winifred Black for King Features Syndicate.

80 Howard was referring to Lookout Mountain specifically, but generally about the Appalachian mountains. It didn't then occur to Howard that Granny Dollar would be the subject of a Winifred Black Story.

81 The upper reaches of DeSoto Falls are characterized by a series of small cascades just below a man-made dam. The cascades drop off a steep precipice creating a 104-foot drop, which crashes loudly into the giant punchbowl known as "the pot hole." In the 1920s, it required some rugged scrambling down a very steep trail to get to the bottom of the falls.

82 On June 3, 1928, more than five months after the Sadie Shrader article was published.

83 The letter from Black actually included two articles, or "sketches" as Howard called them. The second one included a description of Black's trip to Sand Mountain to hear the Pea Ridge singers.

84 Annie Laurie was a pen name that Black used for *The San Francisco Examiner*. The Granny Dollar article appeared on July 1, 1928.

85 Howard's full-page column appeared on page 87 of *The Birmingham News* two months later, on September 9, 1928.

86 Just one year prior, in July 1927, Howard had celebrated the Granny's supposed 101st birthday.

87 Howard correctly ascertained that Granny was born in Georgia, but he reported her birth in Forsyth County. But Forsyth County wasn't formed until December 3, 1831, almost 9 years after Granny's claimed birth. While she may have told Howard that she was born in what was to become Forsyth County, Georgia, it is more likely, as records will show that she was born much later than 1822, after the formation of Forsyth County. And, she was born in neighboring Gwinnett County, Georgia.

88 Howard does not specify that William was a Callahan. However, the context of the writing indicates that William was the father of John Grier Callahan and, therefore, presumably William Callahan.

89 William McIntosh (1775 – April 30, 1825), also known as Tustunnuggee Hutke (White Warrior), was one of the most prominent chiefs of the Wind Clan of the Creek Nation between the turn of the nineteenth century and his execution in 1825. He was a chief of Coweta town in Georgia.

90 This comment about the names of her half-brothers shows the great storytelling ability of Granny Dollar. Although she assigned the humor

to her father and his way of handling names, it is evident, though Howard did not discern it, that this was a fabrication by Granny (as records attest) to add her wit and humor to the story. There are more examples of this storytelling prowess. However, as will be seen, Granny did, indeed, have a sister named Georgia Ann, and a half-sister named Texie Ann.

91 This is a reference to the father of Griffen Callahan b. 1878 in Jackson County, Alabama. He was the son of John B. Callahan. This Callahan family was in Alabama as early as 1815. The line is well-documented, and there is no indication that they are related to Granny Dollar in any way.

92 Howard carelessly referred to Nelson Dollar as "Wilson" Dollar, causing some confusion over the years as to his true name and identity.

"THE FOLKS KEEPS ON COMIN' TO BE CONJURED"

93 Conjuring is a term casually used for well-meaning spiritual healing that has been passed down through generations for hundreds of years. Conjuring is distinct from the practice of healing by the use of herbs, plants, and other natural elements. Conjuring is a supernatural practice akin to faith-healing.

94 Stoney, George C. (director), *All My Babies: A Midwife's Own Story*, Georgia Department of Public Health, *1952*

95 Dunn, Ella Ingenthron, *The Granny Woman of the Hills*, Ozarks Mountaineer; 0th Edition (January 1, 1978)

96 Strayhorn, Zora Shay, McGehee, Jean Devine, McGehee, Charles White, *Mentone Alabama: A History*, Mentone Area Preservation Association, 1986

97 Texas Frances Orleans Johnson and her husband Jesse Johnson were not otherwise related.

98 Strayhorn, et. al.

99 (Hornsby, Sadie B, Sarah H Hall, John N Booth, and Mary Willingham. *I Ain't No Midwife*. Georgia, 1939. Manuscript/Mixed Material. https://www. Loc. Gov/item/wpalh000507/.)

100 In *The Birmingham News* (Birmingham, Alabama), 28 May 1929, Page 4 story, Mrs. W. L. Murdock reported a visit to Granny Dollar's cabin. She stated that Granny, "never learned to read."

101 The local Registrar of beat 28, the area where Granny Dollar lived,

recorded eighteen births for 1925 and twenty-two births for 1924. In five years ending 1925, there were seventy-five births registered.

"...EIGHT MILES EAST OF COFFEETOWN"

102 Howard, Elizabeth, and Kuykendall, James R., *The Montgomery Advertiser*, November 3, 1982, Page 4

   The article introduces and/or reinforces other myths about Granny Dollar. It states that her father was 6'6" and 275 pounds and that multiple wives were "a fairly common" Cherokee practice. One piece of information that Howard reported that is original to Granny Dollar is that her father had a violent temper. This could not have been known by later writers. Records will bear out this description.

103 DeKalb County Resident Larry Chandler recalled his grandmother telling him about a cave known as Callahan's Cave, on Town Creek, that contained a night club, a casino, and a still. This is almost certainly a reference to Sauta Cave and to the legend of Granny Dollar.

104 It is apparent that Granny Dollar originally informed people that she was born on Sand Mountain, "about 8 miles east of Coffeetown," which would describe an area in the middle of the Sand Mountain plateau around the community of Powel. Later, she (or someone else) added the Buck's Pocket location. Buck's Pocket is a natural pocket (canyon) of the Appalachian Mountain chain along South Sauty Creek, an upstream tributary on the east side of Guntersville Lake. Its mouth lies about 4 miles (almost) due south of Langston, Alabama that in an 1837 map, was called Coffee Settlement. (LaTourrette, John *An Accurate Map of the State of Alabama and West Florida*, New York: Colton & Co., 1837)

105 In March 1852, Nelson Dollar, Sr., the future father-in-law of Granny, patented 80 acres in nearby Cherokee County, near Centre, Alabama. He obtained this land under a military warrant, based on his service in Captain Sams' Company, Second Regiment, Georgia Mounted Volunteers, in the Creek ("Florida") War.

106 Cohn, Meredith (October 23, 2015). *"Rare Identical Triplets Born to Baltimore Couple"*. Baltim. Sun. Archived from the original on October 24, 2015. Retrieved October 23, 2015. Indicating the chances 1/1000 of having triplets.

107 In the 1860s, there was a Kyle Auction Store located at the corner of Marietta and Peachtree streets in Atlanta, Georgia.

108 In fact, Granny Dollar was believed to have had brothers and sisters that visited her during the last years of her life. Of particular mention is a brother named Joe Callahan. John Wesley Monroe Dolphus Cooper "Dolphy" was a farm-worker for most of his life in the Ft. Payne/Valley Head area of Alabama. He claimed friendship with the Davenport brothers and Joe Callahan, "the brother of the famous old Indian woman, Granny Dollar" However, as records will show, since the Callahan name was an alias, Granny did not have a brother named Joe Callahan.

109 Thomas Nelson Gray (1886-1960) and his wife, Fannie Morrow (1891-1976) lived in the New Oregon community near Granny Dollar.

"YOU KNOW, I'M AN "INJUN"

110 Examples include Yates, Donald N, *The Bear Went Over the Mountain*, Panther Lodge, 1995; Wilkerson, Lyn, *Slow Travels-Alabama*, Lulu Enterprises Incorporated, 2010; and Rozema, Vicki, *Footsteps of the Cherokees : A Guide to the Eastern Homelands of the Cherokee Nation*, Winston-Salem, N.C. : John F. Blair, 2007.

111 Poorman, Elizabeth, *WHITE LIES, Indigenous Scholars Respond to Elizabeth Warren's Claims to Native Ancestry*, Perspectives on History, American History Association, 2019

112 The final Baker Roll was submitted in 1928. It was compiled using a variety of older rolls, with notations relating to later correspondence. Typed and written on standardized forms, it included the enrollment number (Baker Roll), cross-referenced numbers from the Hester and Churchill Rolls, family name, first name, relationship to the head of the family, sex, age in 1926, date of birth, degree of Cherokee blood, degree of other Indian blood, and remarks. The following earlier rolls were used to compile the final roll:
   1835 Census of Cherokees Living East of the Mississippi River
   1851 Chapman Roll
   1884 Hester Roll
   1907 Council Roll
   1908 Churchill Roll
   1909 Guion Miller Roll

113 2020, *AM I CHEROKEE? CAN I BE PART OF THE EBCI?*, https://e-bci.com/enrollment/ (Note: Blood quantum is calculated from an ancestor listed on the 1924 Baker Roll. DNA testing is not accepted.)

114 Minvielle, Terry, Georgia Recognition of Native American Indians,

House of Representatives Research Office, 1996

115 Waters misstated the name of his mother. She was Mary Lunsford. She was a full Cherokee, who was adopted by the (white) Lunsford family when she was 8 years old.

116 Thornton, Richard. *People of One Fire*. Web. Georgia. 2010-2013.

117 More than 30 individuals from DeKalb County, Alabama, 26 from Gwinnett County, Georgia, and 10 from Forsyth County, Georgia, appear on the Baker Roll. All have western names.

118 Milly Waters and her five children claimed that a clerical error caused them to be left off of the earlier Cherokee rolls. Since she offered no additional evidence, their claim was rejected.

119 Granny Dollar's participation in (claimed) Cherokee rituals, including Cherokee songs, is evident mostly from oral traditions of those who personally knew her. Whether such participation accurately reflected actual Cherokee rituals and rites is not clear.

"...OUT OF MY BABY WAYS"

120 M. Greene, interview by Harriet P. Masters, Johnson City, Tennessee, 10 November 2004. Greene was the granddaughter of a former Southern Appalachian midwife/granny woman, Elizabeth E. Greene. Elizabeth Greene was born prior to 1880. "...now with Grandma, there were stories that her mother was part Indian. But at that time people were real[ly] quiet about being Indian."

121 *The Birmingham News* (Birmingham, Alabama) 22 Jan 1931. Reporting that "Granny Dollar told tourists' fortunes."

"I GOT ME A GOOD MAN"

122 Nancy Dollar claimed to have married only Nelson Dollar, and there is no record of any previous marriage. In 1880, she was recorded in the household of her grandparents (age 32) unmarried. Between 1880 and 1891, it is likely that she remained in the household of her grandparents to care for them. In the 1910 US Census, Nancy reported that she had previously given birth to two children. If this is accurate, she probably had children between the late 1860s and 1880 when she was estranged from her mother's household but prior to living with her grandfather. It is almost certain that these two children were born out of wedlock. As an indication that Nancy remained estranged from her mother, she

NOTES

did not move to Blount County, Alabama, with her other siblings, and instead, remained in Gwinnett County. The only sibling with whom she appears to have had a relationship is her younger sister, California Savannah Callaway Johnson.

123 Nancy and Nelson likely chose to marry in 1909 to ensure that she would receive a pension if he died.

124 It is likely that Nancy was estranged from her mother from an early age. She is last recorded living in the household of her mother at age eleven in 1860. She does not appear in the 1870 census in her mother's household. In 1880, she appears in the household of her grandfather and grandmother. Her grandfather died in 1891, the same year that Nelson Dollar's first wife passed away.

125 Nelson Dollar's birth year is uncertain. He cited his birth year as 1844 in the 1870 US Census. By 1880, he listed his birth year as 1840, and, as time passed, he continued to report his birth year earlier and earlier on US Census records. When he applied for a pension upgrade on account of age in 1906, he reported his birth date as Novembenr 2, 1835. His gravestone lists his birthdate as November 2, 1831. Pension records support the 1835 date. It is likely that he misstated his age when he married a much younger Emily Burton.

126 Nelson Dollar's brother Pinkney was enumerated twice in the 1870 US Census. First, in June, at age 20, living in the household of his brother Nelson, then again (also age 20) in September, in the household of his mother.

127 It is uncertain where Nelson Dollar spent the remainder of the war. He may well have returned to the remote north Georgia mountains to hide out.

128 Nelson Dollar's children were all "of age" by 1899. His youngest son, Oscar Dollar, was recorded in the 1900 US Census (at age 20)living in Sugar Hill, Georgia in the household of his sister Julia and her husband Thomas J. Brown.

129 Application materials for approved claims were retained by the state auditor, which he would use to create a detailed record of pensioners; however, "all applications rejected by the board shall be returned to the county board of examiners, who shall file them with the judge of probate of the county, to be kept for future reference"

"MY FATHER'S HUT WAS ENJOYED BY ALL"

130 Callaway is not consistently spelled in the record. It has been variously spelled Callaway, Calaway, Caloway, and Calloway in the numerous records.

131 The name Callahan is only documented in one record, the marriage of Nelson Dollar and Nancy in 1909. It is not clear why Granny chose the name of Callahan, but it is possible that she chose it because it was similar to her own name and uncommon in the area.

132 There were likely more Callaway orphans, however, their names are not certain at this time.

133 William may have been born in Onslow County, North Carolina prior to his family migrating to Wilkes County, Georgia in 1783.

134 William Callaway's will mentions no wife or children, but only his brothers and sisters. It is likely that he was widowed by this time and that he had made arrangements already for the care of his children.

135 John Callaway, Sr., the uncle of William, had an estate of more than 2,000 acres in Wilkes County, Georgia. The Callaway orphans may well have been shopped around to other related families as well. They eventually came of age in Jasper County, where another set of cousins, including Noah Callaway, had settled. Nancy Dollar had said that her great-great-grandmother had remarried Hugh Holland after the death of William. This is unproven.

136 John Callaway, the son of John Callaway, Sr., had three sons of his own. In the 1820 US Census, he appears in Putnam County, with six sons under the age of 20 in his household.

137 Callaway family researcher Cheri McGuire has said that a lady who lived across the road from where John and Elizabeth Calloway are buried, told her that there was a baby buried there along with them and that it is believed that mental illness ran in Elizabeth's family.

138 William A. Callaway is also known as William Anderson Callaway. However, no record unambiguously gives his middle name. His middle name may be recorded in the Callaway Bible, which was at one time in the possession of Ruby Handley Arons (a great-niece of Granny Dollar) until her death in Blount County, Alabama, in 2005. However, the name Anderson is barely legible, and "Anderson" may not be an accurate reading of his middle name. It is possible, however, that he is named after William Anderson, a prominent and distinguished Revolutionary War

soldier from Wilkes County, Georgia. Also, his great-great-grandmother was named Elizabeth Anderson.

139   Many researchers carry William A. Callaway's birthplace as Gwinnett County. However, his father and mother were married in Jasper County, Georgia in March 1823 and his brother Martin K. Callaway was living there in 1830.

140   Flanigan, J. C., Gwinnett Churches, *A Complete History of Every Church in Gwinnett County, Georgia With Short Biographical Sketches Of Its Ministers*, [Publisher unknown.], 1911

141   The Gwinnett Herald reported on May 7, 1873, that 80 acres of the Callaway tract was being auctioned off by the Sheriff. Leon J. Johnson, the great-grandson of California Callaway wrote that William had 90 slaves and that "life was grand" for his great grandmother. "California grew up not wanting much in life, they lived well in those days. Her father enlisted in the Confederate Army and left them to be on their own. George, her brother, was born in 1863 during the civil war and James was born after the war in 1868. I'm sure mary [sic] had done her best while William was away, but [the] Georgia area was hit hard during the Civil war. They were just 15 miles from Atlanta, Ga., many plantations were lost, and her grandfather, John Callaway, had lost his plantation as many other plantation owners had."

142   By the end of the Civil War, several men owned large tracts near Buford, Georgia. Most of them had been slave owners. These included:William Scales, Benjamin M. Bagby, Willis Benson, James M. Dodd, Jacob Moulder, John Calloway, William Garner, Burton C. Cloud, George and Noah Brogdon, Isham Born, Daniel O. Born, Harrison R. Brogdon, and Hope J. Brogdon. John Callaway's great-grandfather had been a slave owner in Wilkes County, GA, but, there is no indication that John Callaway was ever a slaveholder.

143   The Callaways owned 125 acres of lot 349 (the original lottery grant), 62 1/2 acres of lot 371 (original grant to Jethro Holland), 125 acres of lot 363 (original grant of Matthew Carter). and 62 1/2 acres of lot 361 (original grant to Robert Brown), all in district 7 and clustered around the original grant. This land was collectively known as the "John Callaway home place."

144   Granny Dollar had accurately reported her parents' names as William and Mary Sexton but had intentionally altered the last name from Callaway

to Callahan.

145 Gwinnett County, Georgia Deed Book 13, page 144, dated January 19, 1900

146 Her birth date is carried by some researchers as January 1822 (as listed in the 1900 US Census). However, since her parents were not married until March 1822, it is assumed that she was born in January 1823. Also noted is that her birth year coincides with Nancy Callaway's claimed birth year closely.

"MY BROTHERS AND SISTERS ARE ALL DEAD"

147 She was named Matilda after her great uncle Martin's daughter, Catherine Matilda Callaway, who was her senior by eight years.

148 She was named for her mother and her grandmother Callaway,

149 She was named after her maternal grandmother, Nancy Driskill.

150 She was named after great-aunt Sarah Driskill, and her great grandmother Sarah Collar Callaway.

151 She was named after cousin Frances Caroline Callaway, the daughter of Martin Callaway

152 This was in the area where Granny Dollar would live from 1923 until her death in 1931.

153 William A. Callaway had two sons (half-brothers) named William. The first, William Asbury Callaway is referred to as William Asbury Callaway in this book. The second, William S. Callaway, is referred to as Will Callaway.

154 He was named after his Great Grandfather George Driskill.

155 An interesting note is that the family of Nancy's husband, Nelson Dollar lived close to the Callaway family and the two families share many names. For example, the Dollars used the names Matilda, Noah, Emeline (or Emily), George, and Nancy. Also, the name Tempe (Temperence) exists in both families. So, it is possible that Nelson Dollar and Nancy Callaway were distantly related. Nelson Dollar's mother, both grandmothers, and his maternal grandfather are uncertain. More research will possibly resolve this question.

156 This is a family legend. It isn't actually certain when William Callaway left. But, it was very soon after the end of the war.

157 William A. Callaway's daughter Milly Callaway appears in some records under the name of Milly Cowen.

"MY FATHER WAS A BIG MAN"

158 Deed Book O, page 143, March 29, 1865.

159 Mary Garret Callaway's youngest child, James Noah Callaway died in Colorado City, Texas on July 11, 1952. On the death certificate, his birthdate is listed as March 4, 1872. William Callaway had left the family, finally, in March 1865, almost a full seven years before that purported date of birth. So, either James Noah Callahan was not William's son, or the date of birth listed on his death certificate is wrong. Perhaps both are wrong. It is certain that, at a minimum, the birthdate is wrong. Because "Noah Callaway" appears in the 1870 US Census (documented on September 22, 1870) living in the household of his mother Mary Callaway in Gwinnett County, Georgia as age 3, being born in 1867. The 1900 US Census, shows "Jamie N. Callaway" living in Blount County, Alabama, in the household of his elder brother, Asbury Callaway. That census documents his birth as March 1868. By 1910, the census shows James, still in Blount County, as age 45, being born in 1865. In 1920, James was living in Mitchell Texas, and was listed as age 50, being born in 1870. In 1930, he was listed as age 61, being born in 1869. Finally, the 1940 Census shows James as age 72, being born in 1868. Assuming that William was the father of James, it is most likely that he was born on March 4, 1865, 25 days before William transferred his property to Mary and deserted his family for good.

"...AND SOON THEY ARE DEAD"

160 Some newspapers reported that a third Callaway, called "Jules" was arrested, but this is not supported by the evidence. The name 'Jules' may be a mistaken pronunciation of Ulysses' who was called 'Ule.' In any case, reports are consistent that the two oldest Callaway boys were arrested and taken to Dahlonega, and then Atlanta by federal authorities.

161 The charge was referred to as "adultery."

162 The earlier charges had been federal charges for robbery of a US Post Office and were adjudicated in Federal Court in Atlanta, GA.

163 Two of these men, Thomas Lunsford, and William Seabolt would belong to families related to William Callaway by marriage. George Gurly was the father-in-law of Fulton Williams, who was, in turn, the brother of

Marion Williams.

164 Leon J. Johnson wrote that, according to California Callaway, John and Elizabeth Callaway never knew what happened to their son, William, but this is not supported by the evidence. William's presence in Union County was prominently published and discussed in the local Gwinnett and Atlanta newspapers, and his death was widely reported across Georgia.

165 Illegal bootleg whisky distillers.

166 *The Atlanta Constitution*, Atlanta, Georgia, June 06, 1889 & *Columbus Enquirer-Sun* June 08, 1889.

167 Elijah Henry "Lige" Seabolt was the father-in-law of Thomas Lee Callaway, who married his daughter Susan in July 1890.

168 This is probably Aaron Washington Woody. Newspaper accounts say that, upon receiving the first fire from William S. Callaway, Woody disappeared leaving the two other men to finish the battle.

"I'M COMING TO SEE YOU EVERY DAY."

169 Paton Monroe Lowman was also known as Lafayette Lowman, but claimed that he had no idea how the name Lafayette got attached to his name. However, he had a son named Lafayette and it is likely that their repetitive appearances in Dawson County Courts had led to the confusion.

170 The Lowman jury deliberated for more than 16 hours before reaching a verdict, demonstrating the difficulty of convicting someone for a violent murder in northern Georgia at this time. In his appeal, Lowman's lawyers presented evidence that the judge had erred by allowing prosecutors to inform the jury that Morgan Lowman had reported a still to revenue agents. Since Lowman claimed that he struck his brother-in-law in self-defense, it is evident that Lowman had been accused by Anderson of reporting him to revenue agents and that Anderson had possibly threatened Lowman. One of the jury members was openly hostile to informers and the community generally held informers in such contempt that The Supreme Court of Georgia ruled that this evidence, while it had no impact on the facts of murder itself (there were a dozen eye-witnesses), unfairly prejudiced the defendant and the Court ordered a new trial.

171 Morgan Lowman claimed to have arrived in the Jackson County area of Alabama around 1900. The 1900 US Census shows this Lowman branch

NOTES

living in Cartecay, Gilmer County, Georgia.

172 Neither the Dollars nor the (William) Abbots appeared in the US Census in 1920. According to Floyd Abbot, they were living in the area of Brow Road in the Phillips area (just north of Crow Gap) of Lookout Mountain about 5 miles north of Mentone. It is believed that they were living off of modern-day County Route 734. Neighboring farms along Brow Road, include that of Samuel Goins, Morgan Lowman, Hewan Converse, Walter Hartline, John Richards, Thomas Clinton, Joe Webb, and Benjamin York. Also nearby, was the farm of John Abbot, William Abbot's father. Testimony in the trial of Morgan Lowman indicates that the John Abbot home was about 1 mile from where William Abbot was living (near Granny Dollar). It is evident that the census taker worked along the brow road area and simply missed (or skipped) the entire area of modern-day County Route 734.

173 The Abbots would later demonstrate the reluctance to call an outside physician.

In the 1920s, midwives often provided prenatal care and certainly provided better postnatal care than doctors of the day.

174 Alabama, Convict Records, 1886-1952, Volume 10: 1920-1923 - "Morg" Lowman, a notorious bootlegger, a 70-year-old, was convicted of 2nd-degree manslaughter and served six years in the Alabama Penitentiary.

175 *Lowman v. State*, 18 Ala. App. 569, 93 So. 69 (Ala. Crim. App. 1922)

William Abbot and Morgan Lowman, while drinking moonshine, began to quarrel, apparently over an automobile that was having trouble on the road near their homes. The subsequent assault was witnessed by Abbot's father John Abbot, Pate Lowman's wife (Morgan Lowman's daughter-in-law), and Clara Abbot's step-father, William Pearl Sharp. Witnesses testified that Lowman struck Abbot at least five times with a large seasoned oak stick. At trial, Lowman claimed that his blows did not cause Abbot's death, but instead that Abbot died from drinking moonshine containing lye. At trial, Lowman's attorneys also unsuccessfully argued that it was the family's lack of care, rather than the blows that he delivered, that caused the death. The court said, "The fact that no physician was sent for to attend the injured man cannot avail the defendant, for when death is caused by a dangerous wound, the person inflicting it is responsible for the consequences. The court said, "There was nothing to show that the whisky, drunk by the deceased, contained

Iye.

176 Sometime between January 1920, when the Sharps were living at Cedar Grove, Walker County, Georgia, and shortly after September, when Clara Abbot moved in with them, they moved from a rented farm in Cedar Grove to one in Battelle on the opposite (Western) side of Lookout Mountain.

177 Chambers, John G., *The Times Journal*, Fort Payne, Alabama, 1999

"FOLKS COMES AND HELPS ME, BUT I'M TIRED NOW"

178 James Floyd Cordell was a 21-year-old farm laborer in New Oregon in 1931. He was the son of Joseph Edmund Cordell (1873-1944) and Martha Ellis (1880-1969). Floyd died in Louisville, Kentucky in 2009.

179 Published accounts state that Joseph Cordell's son was also named Joseph. However, this was likely James Floyd Cordell.

180 This was David Lemuel Karl Keith (1877-1946) a farmer in New Oregon in 1931. His wife was Susan Matilda Crow.

181 John Edward Gilliam (1911-1987), one of the sons of Dee Gilliam mentioned above.

182 James Mason "Uncle Doc" White, a prominent (72-year-old) Valley Head minister, sawmill operator, lumberman, and gin operator. He was the preacher at nearby Rock Bridge Church.

183 Velma Frances Kerby (1908-1983) was the daughter of Mentone farmer Louis Bailey Kerby and his wife Maggie Crow.

"...TO KNOW THEM AND THEIR SECRET WAYS."

184 By 1923, Dink Gilliam was working on the road crew working at Wade's Gap.

About the Author

The writer is a native of DeKalb County, Alabama and Chattanooga, Tennessee. He is a 25+ year veteran special agent of the FBI (retired). He lives with his wife (with two sons nearby) in Ooltewah, Tennessee.

www.ingramcontent.com/pod-product-compliance
Lightning Source LLC
Chambersburg PA
CBHW070534090426
42735CB00013B/2983